Metacognition, Worldviews and Religious Education

Religious Education (RE) holds a unique place within the state education system. Yet, the teaching of RE has often been criticised for its tendency to present simplified and stereotypical representations of religions. Bringing together the theory of metacognition with RE curriculum content, this book offers a coherent and theoretically supported approach to RE and beyond that is applicable to a range of subjects and students of various age groups.

Metacognition, Worldviews and Religious Education seeks to support teachers in creating a new and exciting classroom approach. With a focus on putting children and teachers' worldviews back on the RE agenda and developing awareness of these through metacognitive processes, it includes

- Tables, frameworks and checklists to make it easy for teachers to adapt the approach to their own context
- Concrete examples of how the approach can work in the classroom, including case studies from teachers
- Call-out boxes for teachers and others to reflect on their own practice and to consider their own beliefs and values in relation to teaching and learning

Co-authored by three researchers from Exeter University and one experienced advanced skills RE primary school teacher, this book explains in a jargon-free way the theories of metacognition and worldviews which underpin the creation of a unique learning environment, making it an essential read for students, experienced teachers, researchers in RE and anyone interested in taking a thinking skills approach to pedagogy.

Shirley Larkin is a Senior Lecturer in Education at the University of Exeter.

Rob Freathy is Associate Dean of the College of Social Sciences and International Studies at the University of Exeter and Professor of Education in the Graduate School of Education.

Jonathan Doney is a researcher at the University of Exeter specialising in the history and development of education policy, with a focus on Religious Education.

Giles Freathy is the Primary Initial Teacher Training Curriculum Lead for The Learning Institute at the Westcountry Schools Trust.

Metacognition, Worldviews and Religious Education

A Practical Guide for Teachers

SHIRLEY LARKIN, ROB FREATHY,
JONATHAN DONEY AND GILES FREATHY

LONDON AND NEW YORK

First published 2020
by Routledge
2 Park Square, Milton Park, Abingdon, Oxon OX14 4RN

and by Routledge
52 Vanderbilt Avenue, New York, NY 10017

Routledge is an imprint of the Taylor & Francis Group, an informa business

© 2020 Shirley Larkin, Rob Freathy, Jonathan Doney and Giles Freathy

The right of Shirley Larkin, Rob Freathy, Jonathan Doney and Giles Freathy to be identified as authors of this work has been asserted by them in accordance with sections 77 and 78 of the Copyright, Designs and Patents Act 1988.

All rights reserved. No part of this book may be reprinted or reproduced or utilised in any form or by any electronic, mechanical, or other means, now known or hereafter invented, including photocopying and recording, or in any information storage or retrieval system, without permission in writing from the publishers.

Trademark notice: Product or corporate names may be trademarks or registered trademarks, and are used only for identification and explanation without intent to infringe.

British Library Cataloguing-in-Publication Data
A catalogue record for this book is available from the British Library

Library of Congress Cataloging-in-Publication Data
A catalog record has been requested for this book

ISBN: 978-0-367-22304-5 (hbk)
ISBN: 978-0-367-22305-2 (pbk)
ISBN: 978-0-429-27435-0 (ebk)

Typeset in Dante and Avenir
by Deanta Global Publishing Services, Chennai, India

Contents

List of tables	vi
About the authors	vii
Acknowledgements	ix
Introduction	1
1 Creating a metacognitive environment	14
2 Meta-thinking zone	26
Teacher voice 1: Creating a meta-thinking zone in my RE classroom (Helen) 39	
3 The worldview zone	41
Teacher voice 2: Promoting children's views of the world (Jeanette) 55	
4 Resources zone and lesson planning	57
5 A practitioner's approach	70
Teacher voice 3: A teacher's view of using the lessons (Cari) 83	
6 The project and assessment	85
Teacher voice 4: Teachers' views of being involved in the RE-flect project 98	
7 Pupils and teachers developing metacognition	100
8 Conclusion	113
Bibliography	125
Index	129

Tables

1.1	Elements of a metacognitive learning environment	25
2.1	Metacognitive knowledge cards	31
2.2	Monitoring and control cards	32
2.3	Metacognitive experience cards	33
3.1	Worldview Question Framework (WQF) 1	45
3.2	WQF 2	46
3.3	WQF 3	46
3.4	WQF 4	47
3.5	WQF 5	47
4.1	Lesson planning framework checklist	66
7.1	Metacognitive strategy	101
7.2	Metacognitive experiences	101
7.3	Metacognitive knowledge	101
7.4	Cognitive strategies and knowledge	101
7.5	Exploration of my spirituality	107
8.1	The three learning dimensions in the RE-flect approach	122

About the authors

Shirley Larkin
I research and write about metacognition across the curriculum and across age ranges. I am interested in how metacognition helps us to learn throughout life. In addition to the RE-flect project, my research on metacognition has covered early years, literacy, numeracy and science. These projects have resulted in a number of book chapters, articles, conference papers and a single authored book, *Metacognition in Young Children* (Routledge, 2010). I am currently a Senior Lecturer in the Graduate School of Education at the University of Exeter.

Rob Freathy
At the University of Exeter, I am Associate Dean of the College of Social Sciences and International Studies, and Professor of Education in the Graduate School of Education. I am co-editor of a series of books published by Peter Lang on the theme of 'Religion, Education and Values'. I have authored and edited numerous books, including *Religious Education and Freedom of Religion and Belief* (Oxford, 2012), *History, Remembrance and Religious Education* (Oxford, 2014) and *Politics, Professionals and Practitioners* (London, 2017).

Jonathan Doney
I am a researcher at the University of Exeter specialising in the history and development of education policy, with a focus on Religious Education. I have been involved in a number of classroom-based research projects and have previously taught RE at primary and secondary schools, and have been involved in Initial Teacher Training of RE teachers.

Giles Freathy
I am the Primary Initial Teacher Training Curriculum Lead for The Learning Institute at the Westcountry Schools Trust. Formerly an Advanced Skills Teacher and Specialist Leader of Education for Religious Education, Humanities and Thinking Skills, I was the recipient of the TES Humanities Award (2014). I have been on the steering group for the 'Learn Teach

Lead RE' project in the South West and Cornwall SCARE's professional RE consultant. I am also Chair of the board of directors for Connect Academy Trust in Plymouth.

Helen

I qualified as a Primary School Teacher in 1997 and worked full time as a Primary Class Teacher in Key Stage 2 until 2005. I returned after a year to work part time after a maternity break to teach RE across Key Stage 1 (5–7-year-olds) and Key Stage 2 as PPA cover for four years. A change of teaching direction led me to train in Every Child Counts maths intervention, and I continue to work in a school teaching maths as an intervention.

Jeanette

Following a move to Devon in 1993, I changed my career path from School Secretary to Teaching Assistant. The school was very forward-thinking, so encouraged me to extend my knowledge and experience by taking several specialist courses. After being awarded the Higher-Level Teaching Assistant status, I was asked to cover PPA (planning, preparation and assessment) sessions, teaching a variety of subjects but mainly Religious Education. In addition, I assisted the Religious Education coordinator with planning and continuing professional development sessions. When I retired in 2017, my job role had progressed to covering any member of the Key Stage 2 (7–11-year-old) teaching staff whilst they were absent.

Cari

In 2001, I gained my Bachelor of Education in Primary Education with Art and Design, having previously worked as a Teaching Assistant for eight years. I taught in a local school for 13 years across the key stages. Since leaving I have worked as a supply teacher with a specialty in art and also as a freelance artist in schools. Recent work has included work with Church of England schools entitled 'The Saints Project', which successfully explored saints attached to each school and the meaning of sainthood through art.

Acknowledgements

We would like to thank all the teachers and pupils who worked with us on the RE-flect project over the two years. We are grateful to you all for allowing us access to your classrooms and for sharing with us your thoughts throughout the project. This book can only give a snapshot of some of the great material you co-created with us during the two years, but without your enthusiasm and commitment, the RE-flect project would have remained an idea in the imagination of a group of researchers. Thank you for bringing it to realisation.

Introduction

Religious Education (RE) is currently facing challenging times. Some of these challenges are legal and policy-related, concerning the control and organisation of RE. Some are rooted in deficiencies in terms of human resourcing and funding. Some are grounded in the study of religion(s), for example, unresolved conceptual, theoretical and methodological debates. Some are reflections of societal and cultural transformations, including changing beliefs, values, practices and identities, as well as the shifting private and public relevance and significance of religious literacy. At the same time as facing these challenges, there have been moves towards revolutionary changes in the nature, purpose and scope of RE, for example the 11 recommendations of the Commission on Religious Education (2018), which was sponsored by the Religious Education Council of England and Wales. This two-year-long Commission collected evidence from 'a wide-range of concerned parties including pupils, teachers, lecturers, advisers, parents and faith and belief communities' (Commission on Religious Education, 2018, p. i). Whilst reception of these recommendations has been mostly positive, an initial response from the British Government was more muted. Further progress is dependent on, amongst other things, an increased consensus and unity across the whole RE community, and a willingness and opportunity within parliamentary processes to draft, discuss, pass and enact any necessary legislation.

This book seeks to address some of the particular pedagogical and curricular challenges and opportunities facing RE at the present time and considered by the Commission on Religious Education. It does so by endorsing an innovative approach to teaching and learning in RE through the creation of a metacognitive learning environment.

As a starting point, this chapter sets out contemporary challenges and issues in RE in schools today and identifies the pedagogical and curricular problems and opportunities which the book seeks to address. Second, the chapter outlines the theoretical framework underpinning the RE-flect project upon which the book is based. It describes the aims and the methods we used on the project to meet the identified challenges, issues and problems.

A brief discussion is also included within this section to emphasise how the principles upon which our pedagogical proposals and procedures are based can be used for all learning, not just in RE and not just in primary schools.

Context

Religious Education (RE) occupies a unique place within the curriculum of state-maintained schools in England. Although it falls outside of the National Curriculum, all schools must make provision for the subject for pupils aged 5–18. The legal framework states that, in state-maintained schools *without* a religious character, RE must *not* be provided by means of any catechism or formulary which is distinctive of a particular religious denomination, and must reflect the fact that the religious traditions in Great Britain are in the main Christian, whilst taking account of the teaching and practices of the other principal religions represented in Great Britain. By contrast, in state-maintained schools with a religious character, RE can be provided in accordance with the tenets of the designated faith. This book is primarily orientated around RE in the first context, but its curricular and pedagogical proposals may also be applicable to RE in faith schools.

The difference between a school with a religious character and one without may be negligible in practice. In theory, however, the difference could be profound. The authority of state-maintained schools without a religious affiliation to determine the truth, credibility or validity of any publicly contested (non-)religious worldview is restricted. To make such a determination would be tantamount to promoting a particular faith position and religious character. RE in such schools has been characterised negatively as 'non-denominational' and/or 'non-confessional'. To uphold the liberal principle and human right of freedom of religion and belief, the curriculum and pedagogy of RE in such schools must not be predicated upon any particular religious or non-religious worldview, philosophy or ideology or arguably any single conceptual, theoretical, interpretative or methodological framework. These all rest on fundamental assumptions about the nature of reality and what can be known about it and how. Inclusive multi-faith RE needs to adopt a procedural agnosticism regarding such claims, a plurality of foundational frameworks and perspectives and a self-conscious and self-critical orientation regarding the assumptions underpinning its aims, methods and selected content.

Within professional and policy discourse, the following challenges, issues and problems have been identified as currently facing RE: ongoing and seemingly irresolvable debates about its nature and purpose; a lack of clear criteria for selecting and sequencing curriculum content; criticism from the inspectorate about the quality of teaching and learning in RE, especially concerns over how the progression of pupils can be assessed; an over-reliance on non-specialist teachers in secondary schools and unqualified teachers in primary schools; cutbacks in teacher training; derisory levels of resourcing and support; inadequate continuing professional development provision; a lack of adequate mechanisms for ensuring school compliance with statutory obligations; and the deconstruction of the local authority structures by which RE has traditionally been determined in state-maintained schools without a religious affiliation. It was to address such matters that the Commission on Religious Education (2018) was established.

In the midst of this purported crisis, a growing number of researchers and practitioners have called for greater attention to be paid to the meaning of, and relationship between, curriculum, pedagogy and assessment. Specifically, there have been demands for greater sophistication in the RE community's handling of issues concerning: the teaching and assessment of content and skills; conceptual and cognitive development; and the personal relevance to pupils of what they are learning and how they should reflect upon and respond to it. The inadequacy of assessment in RE has become a focus, not only in terms of changing methodology (e.g. with or without level descriptors) and unclear attainment targets (e.g. the once near-universal 'learning *about* religions' and 'learning *from* religion'), but also in terms of articulating precise intended learning outcomes. These are rarely expressed in language more sophisticated than 'knowledge and understanding', leading to nebulous notions of the cognitive processes necessary for success. Even where greater precision is evident, how do teachers and pupils conceptualise verbs such as 'interpret', 'evaluate', 'describe', 'explain', 'analyse', 'identify', 'appreciate' and 'appraise'? Is there clarity regarding the subject's contribution to pupils' mental, cognitive and linguistic development? What are the intentions and expectations of teachers in terms of pupil progression and achievement in RE? Another key issue is how to conceptualise the relationship between pupils' own interests and questions on the one hand, and the academic study of religion(s) and worldview(s) on the other. To what extent (if any), and for what reasons, should RE seek to encourage pupils to think about, develop and/or express their own identities, beliefs and values?

In addressing such matters, RE researchers have tended to focus upon subject-specific pedagogical methods (including the principles and procedures of teaching, learning and assessing in RE), whilst RE practitioners have tended to focus upon subject-specific content knowledge (i.e. knowledge and skills appropriated from the academic study of religion(s) and most frequently derived from Theology and Religious Studies). There have been few examples of RE community members drawing upon generic pedagogical and psychological knowledge drawn from educational studies, educational psychology and cognate disciplines. This book attempts just that.

In doing so, it does not orientate itself around the existing canon of research and professional literature or provide an extended critique of established RE pedagogies. There is simply not space to rehearse the history of RE theories and practices. Instead, we seek to set out a new pedagogical strategy for RE in primary schools (i.e. 5–11-year-olds). Only in passing will it be explained how our approach builds upon existing theory and practice. To do otherwise would be to devote too much attention to the rear-view mirror and not enough to the road ahead. Readers interested in locating our approach within the wider landscape of RE curricular and pedagogical theories and practices may wish to read more widely.

We can say, however, that our 'metacognitive approach' is informed by the following overarching assumptions, which underlie the more specific pedagogical principles utilised on the RE-flect project. Inclusive multi-faith RE should teach pupils about religion(s) and worldview(s) as significant components of human existence in the past, present and probable future. As the Commission on Religious Education states:

> Young people today are growing up in a world where there is increasing awareness of the diversity of religious and non-religious worldviews, and they will need to live and work well with people with very different worldviews from themselves … Knowledge of religious and non-religious worldviews is an essential part of all young people's entitlement to education [regardless of their background, personal beliefs or the type of school they attend].
>
> (2018, p. 3)

By developing such knowledge, understanding and skills, they learn to 'engage with important aspects of human experience including the religious, spiritual, cultural and moral'; they gain 'insight into the sciences, the arts, literature, history and contemporary local and global social and political issues'; and they 'develop greater respect and empathy for others' and the ability 'to deal positively with controversial issues, to manage strongly held differences of belief and to challenge stereotypes' (Commission on Religious Education 2018, p. 5).

Another assumption is that RE should not seek to promote religious or non-religious beliefs, practices and allegiances, even whilst encouraging pupils to reflect upon the subject matter from their own points of view. The controversial nature of the beliefs and practices encountered in RE means that the stakes involved in determining the subject's aims, methods and contents are probably higher than they are with regard to any other curriculum subject. A desire for fairness and balance is a pre-requisite, but so, in our opinion, should be a yearning for transparency and openness in curricular and pedagogical decision-making processes in RE. This can only be achieved if pupils are invited to participate in the kinds of discussion that were traditionally the preserve of those theorists, curriculum designers and teachers who pre-determined the subject outside of the classroom. For pupils, this means learning to engage in dialogue about what is taught in RE (i.e. contents), why (i.e. aims) and how (i.e. methods). As the Commission on Religious Education has stated:

> Pupils must be taught the different ways in which religion and worldviews can be understood, interpreted and studied, including through a wide range of academic disciplines [e.g. anthropology, area studies, hermeneutics, history, other human and social sciences, philosophy, religious studies and theology] and through direct encounter and discussion with individuals and communities who hold these worldviews.
>
> (2018, p. 13)

Thereby, they 'experience a range of academic approaches to the nature, origin, role and function of religious and non-religious worldviews in people's lives' (2018, p. 37).

It is to this end that we believe the main purpose of RE should be to teach pupils the disciplinary knowledge and skills associated with the communities of academic inquiry concerned with the study of religion(s) and worldview(s), for example, through theological and religious studies ('non-confessional' forms of theological studies promote the study of God, or the concept of God, in the context of studying theistic religions, and are open to scholars of all religious and non-religious persuasions). The academic study of religion(s) and worldview(s) is not simply characterised by the accumulation of knowledge about religion(s) and worldview(s) but embraces learning how to participate in ongoing dialogues between those who generate, disseminate, use and critique such knowledge. Dialogue partners include those representing multiple disciplines and a plurality of philosophical and theoretical frameworks. In the context of RE, this multi-perspectival complexity is borne out in a plethora of possible pedagogical approaches, each reflecting different assumptions about the nature of religions and worldviews, what we can know about them and how we should study them. The complexity and diversity are tangible at the level of:

1. Disciplinary skills, 'including qualitative and quantitative research skills (at age appropriate levels), philosophical enquiry, hermeneutical approaches to texts, and approaches for understanding the arts, rituals, practices and other forms of expression' (Commission on Religious Education, 2018, p. 77), and
2. Transferable skills: 'analysing a range of primary and secondary sources, understanding symbolic language, using technical terminology effectively, interpreting meaning and significance, empathy, respectful critique of beliefs and positions, recognizing bias and stereotype, and representing views other than one's own with accuracy' (Commission on Religious Education, 2018, p. 29).

On the RE-flect project, to avoid promoting any particular ontological and/or epistemological assumptions over others, in the distinctive context of so-called 'non-confessional' and 'non-denominational' RE in schools without a religious affiliation, we did not advocate the use of a singular specialised methodology or method for studying religion(s) and worldview(s). Instead, we promote a plurality of pedagogies for teaching about religion(s) and worldview(s), albeit always within the context of a 'metacognitive learning environment'. Such an approach recognises that, in terms of religious or philosophical foundations, no common goal or common ground can be assumed. It is not the responsibility of RE teachers to promote any particular theory or definition of religion(s) or worldview(s), or a specific methodology or method for studying religion(s) and worldview(s). Instead, it is to facilitate pupils' awareness, discussion and evaluation of the significance and effectiveness of multiple disciplinary methodologies and methods, and a plurality of the pedagogies of RE to which they give rise. Here our assumption is that any methodological and/or pedagogical approach would be enhanced if its nature and purpose became an explicit focus of thought and discussion, especially if this was combined on the part of pupils with an awareness of themselves and of their own cognitive processes.

There is no neutral vantage point from which religions and worldviews can be explored without prejudice, but we can seek to acknowledge our biases and recognise the distinctiveness of our own and other people's perspectives. The result is not objectivity, but intersubjectivity and epistemological and methodological humility. The strategy for attaining this level of reflexivity is in one sense simple: reflection. Reflection on what is learnt about religion(s) and worldview(s); reflection on how to learn about religion(s) and worldview(s); and reflection on oneself as a learner learning about religion(s) and worldview(s). Thereby, at a conceptual level appropriate for their age, pupils might learn to participate in conversations about the nature of religion(s) and worldview(s), how knowledge about religion(s) and worldview(s) is produced and the skills and dispositions associated with those who study religion(s) and worldview(s). Every aspect of classroom RE, including the teacher and the learners, should arguably be within the sightlines of pupils' reflections. Thus, at different points in time, windows become lenses through which objects are viewed; windows become objects to be viewed; and windows become mirrors in which the pupils see themselves.

As this chapter and book proceed, it will be seen how our overarching assumptions about the nature and purpose of RE influenced, but did not dictate, the more specific pedagogical principles and procedures adopted on the RE-flect project. These were devised deliberately to be acceptable to a professional audience with a wider-ranging set of assumptions.

The RE-flect project

This book is aimed at primary school teachers, teacher trainers, teacher trainees, researchers and others who are interested in RE. It is an outcome of a research project called *RE-flect: A programme to foster metacognition in the Religious Education classroom*, which was funded by The Esmée Fairbairn Foundation. The project was undertaken by researchers in the University of Exeter's Graduate School of Education in collaboration with six teacher volunteers. It sought to support the teachers in creating a new and exciting approach to RE in primary schools, specifically by turning their classrooms into metacognitively oriented learning environments. In so doing, it promoted principles and procedures of teaching and learning, based on generic pedagogical and psychological knowledge, that are capable of being deployed as a complement to (almost) any existing RE-specific pedagogy (regardless of its particular ontological, epistemological and methodological foundation). This is primarily because our pedagogical principles and procedures are neither predicated upon singular theories, interpretations, methodologies and methods deployed in the study of religion(s) and worldview(s) nor focused on particular bodies of subject-specific content knowledge appropriated from Theology, Religious Studies or cognate disciplines.

The RE-flect project was based on Flavell's (1979) theory of metacognition. He defined metacognition as everything we know and believe about our own cognitive processes and those of others and the regulation and control of thinking processes. Flavell's original rationale for developing metacognition was not only that pupils would comprehend and learn better in formal educational settings, but 'make wise and thoughtful life decisions' now as children and later as adults (Flavell 1979, p. 910). For Flavell, it is the cognitive process of making conscious decisions and the metacognitive awareness of this process that is important, rather than only the content of those decisions. Through facilitating pupils' metacognition and critical reflection on their beliefs and values, as well as fostering inter-active, mutually-supportive learning about religion(s) and worldview(s), the RE-flect project was the first to apply metacognitive theory to RE in English schools.

There are few existing examples of researchers focusing upon metacognition in relation to RE in other contexts or to similar areas of study. Here we outline just two illustrative cases. First, recognising the importance that pupils' beliefs about knowledge, knowing and learning have over learning processes and outcomes, Theo van der Zee and others (2006) researched metacognitive beliefs about RE amongst pupils in Catholic primary schools in the Netherlands. This included studying pupils' beliefs about:

- The 'realistic' content of RE, i.e. whether it is perceived to be anchored in a historical, social and cultural context, and relates to real-life situations beyond school;
- The role of other people in RE, including those who are physically present (e.g. other pupils) or are represented (e.g. the storied other, for example, in biblical narratives);
- The self and personal motivation in relation to the specific domain (e.g. pupils' willingness to learn, their valuation of content and their perceived control of and competence in learning activities); and
- The teacher's role, including their cognitive, motivational and affective functions (i.e. allowing, motivating and valuing pupil participation).

The researchers also investigated the extent to which social differences between pupils (e.g. religious self-definition and beliefs, participation in religious practices and parental religiosity) influenced their metacognitive beliefs. The study concluded by positing seven categories of inter-related metacognitive beliefs about RE amongst the project participants.

Second, working in the context of St Mary's University (Halifax, Canada), Shelagh Crooks and Alexander Soucy (2015) promoted the development of metacognition amongst undergraduate students of Religious Studies. Their assumption was that those who are metacognitively aware of how they are processing new information are better able to take strategic control over their learning and to plan, monitor, evaluate and even revise their thinking. For Crooks and Soucy, metacognition is comprised of two distinct, but connected activities or functions: (1) the monitoring of cognition; and (2) the regulation of cognition through the purposeful deployment of cognitive strategies. As an alternative to developing metacognitive awareness by fostering 'reflective discourse environments' in which students' thinking is made an on-going 'meta-theme', Crooks and Soucy set students in a senior Religious Studies seminar the complex and consequential problem of designing a new course on an unfamiliar topic that is rarely addressed in Religious Studies. This course would subsequently be taught to undergraduate students who are at an earlier stage of the same degree programme. Consequently, the student participants would undertake 'curriculum reading', first as learners (inquiry-focused), then as course designers (problem-focused). Successful completion of this intellectual and practical task would demand purposeful and strategic metacognitive reading and thinking (including, for example, assessing the significance, relevance and veracity of the assertions and interpretations contained within the literature); the identification, monitoring and evaluation of personal responses to the relevant material (including, for example, analysing and reflecting on the students' own thoughts and feelings, and how these might be influencing the processes of curriculum reading and designing); and careful consideration of the thinking and learning of their junior peers, to further inform the selection and sequencing of material, so as to create a comprehensive, coherent and contextually-appropriate curriculum. In conclusion, they believe their approach promoted metacognition but also student engagement, a sense of responsibility to other students and an environment of equality.

The two earlier examples alone highlight the range of specific topics upon which research on metacognition in RE and Religious Studies can focus, including, for example, metacognitive beliefs about knowledge, knowing, self and others; metacognitive reading, learning and thinking; and metacognitive monitoring and regulation. In relation to such ideas, the RE-flect project sought to address some of the difficulties currently faced by primary school RE teachers. It was hoped, for example, that the approach would help RE teachers think more carefully about pupils' (meta)cognitive development; the relationship between pedagogical knowledge, processes of learning and subject content knowledge; and how to facilitate deeper engagement with key concepts, beliefs and practices. It was also hoped that pupils would come to see that curriculum resources and the narratives that interconnect them were not a 'given' but were respectively selected, sequenced and imposed by the teacher, syllabus designer, textbook writer and so on. Thereby the project sought simultaneously to place learners at the heart of the learning process whilst building a bridge between the learner and the curriculum content.

By increasing the quantity and quality of pupil's metacognitive knowledge and monitoring skills, it was assumed that learners would be better able: to distinguish between understanding and not understanding things; to explain why they do (not) feel puzzled, confused and uncertain about a specific task or new knowledge; and/or to identify the variables that are facilitating or inhibiting their learning. In a subject where pupils may experience emotional reactions to the curriculum content about which they are learning, it was also assumed that metacognition could better enable pupils to monitor and self-regulate their thinking so as to permit in-depth comprehension and engagement, as well as the critical appraisal of what (if any) messages they should believe and act upon.

The research questions guiding the RE-flect project were as follows:

1. What is the impact of creating metacognitively oriented classroom environments on attainment in RE in participating schools?
2. What is the impact of creating metacognitively oriented RE classrooms on participating pupils' perceptions of their learning environment?
3. How was metacognition demonstrated by pupils during RE-flect activities?
4. Does 'worldview profiling' facilitate participating pupils' reflection on, and articulation of, their worldviews both in isolation from, and in relation to, the worldviews of others?

With regard to the last research question, as well as encouraging pupils to think about and monitor their own thinking and learning in RE, the RE-flect project interpreted metacognition in the widest sense, including self-understanding of one's own personal identity, ultimate/existential beliefs, ontology and epistemology, values and ethical principles.

The project thus promoted the provision of opportunities for pupils in RE lessons to identify, reflect on, monitor and develop their own worldviews. The Commission on Religious Education (2018, p. 4) defined worldviews as follows:

> The English word "worldview" is a translation of the German *weltanschauung*, which literally means a view of the world. A worldview is a person's way of understanding, experiencing and responding to the world. It can be described as a philosophy of life or an approach to life. This includes how a person understands the nature of reality and their own place in the world. A person's worldview is likely to influence and be influenced by their beliefs, values, behaviours, experiences, identities and commitments.
>
> We use the term "institutional worldview" to describe organised worldviews shared among particular groups and sometimes embedded in institutions. These include what we describe as religions as well as non-religious worldviews … . We use the term "personal worldview" for an individual's own way of understanding and living in the world, which may or may not draw from one, or many, institutional worldviews.

By ascertaining a greater awareness of their own personal worldviews, it was assumed that pupils would come to appreciate that they held particular assumptions about the nature of reality and what can be known about it, and that these assumptions may not be the same as those of others. By recognising that their (non-)religious positioning was not only bounded and limited, but contingent upon particular personal experiences and assumptions, it was hoped that pupils would become increasingly open to learning about alternative positions, predicated on different experiences and assumptions. Metacognition would facilitate recognition that one's worldview was a worldview. By reflecting upon it in the light of possible alternatives, pupils would arguably become more open to learning about contested truth claims and become more capable of responding to them intelligently. Thus, by developing self-awareness, bringing to consciousness the beliefs and values that constitute our worldviews and underpin our actions, it would be possible for pupils to enter into genuine dialogue with those of alternative worldviews, recognising nuances of difference within and between worldviews, as well as the complexity of identity and culture.

Although it was accepted that the whole school experience should enable pupils 'to understand the worldviews of others and reflect on their own', it was also assumed that 'the explicit, rigorous academic study of a wide range of religious and non-religious worldviews [in RE]' would make a particular contribution by teaching pupils 'how worldviews are formed and expressed, how they have changed over time and their influences on various aspects of individual, communal and national life' (Commission on Religious Education, 2018, p. 26–27). Thereby RE provides a distinctive forum in which pupils learn to 'reflect on their own personal responses to the fundamental human questions to which worldviews respond' and 'articulate these responses clearly and cogently while respecting the right of others to differ' (Commission on Religious Education, 2018, p. 77).

To promote metacognition, the RE-flect project needed to create RE classroom environments with psycho-social conditions conducive to a metacognitive orientation.

This necessitated a focus on the beliefs and practices of the classroom community, the key role of language in teaching and learning and the requirement to encourage pupils to reflect on, critique and possibly alter their thinking processes. In RE-flect, this socio-cultural theory of metacognition was put into practice through the creation of three classroom zones:

- Meta-thinking – thinking about thinking and learning in RE (thinking processes)
- Worldview – thinking about myself as a learner in RE (self-awareness)
- Resources – thinking about representations of (non-)religious phenomena in RE (encounter with subject knowledge)

It was with the purpose of creating and evaluating metacognitive learning environments consisting of the three meta-thinking, resources and worldview zones that we recruited six volunteer primary school teachers who were approached via the University of Exeter's initial teacher education partnership and through links with the local authority advisor for RE. The participation of the teachers included attending five 'Teacher Days' (three for the pilot study and two for the main study) where they engaged in reflective discussion with the research team and each other about the aims of the project, the theories and practices we were advocating and their successes and failures of implementing our approach in individual classroom contexts.

The teachers came from different co-educational, mixed-ability, state-maintained primary schools in the South West of England (including two voluntary-controlled Church of England). Four of the teachers worked with classes containing Year 5 pupils only (aged 9–10). One of the teachers worked with a mixed Year 5/6 class, but only data pertaining to the Year 5 pupils was collected. Year 5 was chosen as a special focus because it allowed us to work with children nearing the transition to secondary schooling, whilst also avoiding Year 6 classes, which can be dominated by preparations for national Standard Assessment Tests. The sixth teacher was re-deployed in the second year of the project to a class containing Year 3 pupils only (ages 7–8). The total number of pupils participating in the main study (year two) was 160. In every class, six pupils were selected by the teacher to form focus groups, containing three girl/boy pairs. The paired pupils were interviewed at the beginning and end of the second year about their RE classroom, their RE lessons and their learning in RE.

An initial questionnaire and group discussion enabled an assessment of the current state of RE in the participating schools. All of the schools were supposed to be teaching RE according to their respective Local Education Authority's Agreed Syllabus for RE, but none of them were teaching the agreed syllabi at the start of the project. Provision was often ad hoc, subject to other curriculum demands, and when they occurred, RE lessons often focused on ethical and environmental issues or were devoted to creative artistic activities. Only three of our teachers were the main teachers for the classes to whom they were teaching RE, and none of the teachers were RE specialists. In two of the other schools, a part-time teacher taught all RE across the school, usually when the class teacher was involved in 'planning, preparation and assessment' (PPA) time; the other teacher was employed as a higher level teaching assistant, again, taking responsibility for RE in a number of classes.

From theory to practice: In English RE and beyond

There is growing awareness of the theory of metacognition in the UK. It has long been a part of pedagogy in other European countries and in the USA. Research since the 1970s has shown the academic and educational benefits of facilitating metacognitive development of pupils across subject domains. However, little has been written for teachers that shows how they might create a complete metacognitive learning environment which works in their local context and which facilitates pupils in developing their ability to reflect on their own thinking, beliefs and values.

This book seeks to fill this gap by presenting a coherent and theoretically supported metacognitive approach to RE. Although different countries have varied arrangements for RE in schools, the subject does often take place in one form or another and in one kind of institution or another, so the book is of potential relevance to teachers beyond England, the UK and the anglophone world (Australia, New Zealand, Canada, USA, etc.). Furthermore, whilst focusing on RE, the metacognitive approach herein outlined can easily be transferred to any subject area and to any age group. Moreover, there is some evidence from the project that teachers who created a metacognitive environment in their RE classes carried this approach over into their other teaching. This book provides teachers with a blueprint for creating a metacognitive environment and learning experiences that can be adapted for use across curriculum areas, whilst maintaining a common thread between them. Thus, the book will be useful for all teachers and education professionals interested in the broader area of thinking in education.

One of the primary aims of the book is to provide teachers with guidance about how to create a metacognitive environment in the RE classroom. To this end, with the intention of interweaving theory and practice, one chapter has been written by the advanced practitioner who created many of the project's resources and trialled them in his own classroom, and four 'Teacher Voices' between chapters have been included to give different teachers' views of the pedagogical process. The chapters also include call-out boxes to provoke reader reflection and suggested further reading. Overall, we hope the book steers a satisfactory course between pure theoretical and applied practical knowledge.

Outline of the book

The book contains the seven main chapters outlined in the next section.

Chapter 1, 'Creating a metacognitive environment', provides a brief overview of the theory of metacognition and relates this to classroom practice and learning. It also explains how to establish a metacognitive learning environment. In the RE-flect project, this entailed the creation of three physical zones in the primary RE classroom: (1) meta-thinking zone, (2) worldview zone and (3) resources zone.

Chapter 2, 'Meta-thinking zone', emphasises how the language of thinking contributes to the development of metacognition. It provides a detailed discussion of the way teachers can frame questions and statements so as to develop pupils' reflection on thinking and encourage them to develop their use of reflective language. The purpose is to engender metacognitive knowledge, monitoring, control processes and strategies such as planning and evaluating.

Chapter 3, 'The worldview zone', begins with a critical discussion of academic theories relating to the need for pupils to reflect on their own worldviews in RE and discusses the extent to which these have become embodied in official curriculum documentation. It then introduces the theory and practice of 'worldview profiling' in RE, providing evidence of its successes and failures in curriculum trials as part of the RE-flect project and making recommendations for future policy, practice and research.

Chapter 4, 'Resources zone and lesson planning', focuses on the resources zone within the context of the RE-flect 'Lesson Planning Framework', showing how the project's approach to teaching and learning addresses key issues relating to current practice in RE. The resources zone and the Lesson Planning Framework are explained in sufficient detail so as to enable teachers to create their own RE-flect activities and lessons. A checklist is provided for teachers to use in their planning to ensure they have provided sufficient opportunities for the development of pupils' metacognition.

Chapter 5, 'A practitioner's approach', presents the personal perspective of an advanced classroom practitioner as he went about designing and trailing activities and lessons to exemplify the RE-flect Lesson Planning Framework. Using practical examples, the author discusses the challenge of providing pupils with opportunities both to develop metacognitively and to learn the subject content knowledge demanded by his syllabus. Thereby insights are provided into the rhetoric and reality of curriculum development and the complex process of turning theory into practice.

Chapter 6, 'The project and assessment', provides contextual information about the schools involved in the project and what teachers initially said about the teaching of RE in their schools. A realistic view of how RE is often seen in primary schools and the types of activities provided for this age group are outlined. The chapter goes on to show what the project teachers subsequently came to believe about the opportunities RE can provide to develop pupils' thinking. This discussion is then related to the difficult and complex issue of assessment in RE, the strengths and weaknesses of the types of assessment used in the project and what this told us about the impact of the RE-flect project on pupils' learning in and perceptions of RE.

Chapter 7, 'Pupils and teachers developing metacognition', draws on classroom observations to illustrate what is meant by metacognition in the RE context. A method of observing and evaluating metacognition which can be used across subject areas is given. Examples of pupils' growing knowledge and understanding of RE subject content, as well as their developing awareness of their own thinking, beliefs and values are provided. The chapter also discusses how participating teachers were encouraged to develop their own metacognition through reflection on their own experiences of RE and how this has impacted on their professional practice.

Chapter 8, 'Conclusion', provides a summary of the key elements of the RE-flect approach with reference to the three metacognitive learning environment zones and the Lesson Planning Framework. The chapter summarises the strengths and challenges of the approach and how it might be implemented in any RE classroom. It also explains how the principles might be adapted for use in other phases of education and/or applied across the curriculum. The chapter concludes with some further recommendations for teaching and learning in RE, building on the experiences and findings of the RE-flect project, as well as positing a vision of how the foci of the three metacognitive learning environment zones can be balanced and integrated.

The main chapters are interspersed with Teacher Voices, where three of the RE-flect teachers write about their experience of the project. The fourth Teacher Voice contains the views of other teachers on the project.

In each chapter there are Call-Out boxes providing questions for you to reflect on, and at the end of each chapter we have suggested some further reading. The full reference list of all the works cited in the text is at the end of the book.

Further reading

Clarke, C. and Woodhead, L. (2015) *A New Settlement: Religion and Beliefs in Schools*. Lancaster, UK: Westminster Faith Debates.

Commission on Religious Education. (2018) *Final Report: Religion and Worldviews: The Way Forward*. London: Religious Education Council of England and Wales.

Dinham, A. and Shaw, M. (2015) *RE for REal: The Future of Teaching and Learning about Religion and Belief*. London: Goldsmith, University of London.

Freathy, G., Freathy, R., Doney, J., Walshe, K. and Teece, G. (2015) *The RE-searchers: A New Approach to Primary Religious Education*. Exeter, UK: University of Exeter.

Creating a metacognitive environment

1

What do you do when you are faced with a task? As I am currently trying to write this chapter I am thinking particularly about writing, but you might substitute any other kind of task you are faced with at work or at home. One answer you may give is 'it depends on the task', and you would be right to think so. I will come back to task creation in Chapter 2. For the moment, as I am engaged in writing I will concentrate on this task. An important starting point is to recognise that as I am the one doing the writing, I cannot view 'writing' as something separate from myself. Instead, the act of writing and what I know about myself, my self-concept, become intertwined into a view of myself as a writer. Chandler (1995) suggests that people approach writing in different ways, e.g. some consciously adopt an 'architectural' strategy which involves creating a clear plan, sectioning up the writing, writing and then editing. This is probably the way most of us were taught to write, particularly for non-fiction and academic purposes. Other writers, he suggests, adopt a 'bricklaying strategy', where each sentence or paragraph is worked on until perfect before the writer moves on. Thus, there is little need for final revisions and editing. Yet others employ strategies more akin to visual artists, e.g. an 'oil painting' approach in which writers layer the writing, often deleting whole chunks (painting over) with little planning; these writers write to understand their thinking rather than to report it; in contrast, those who take a 'water colourist approach' attempt to complete the writing without revision, staying true to 'an inner voice' and keeping the spontaneity of the writing.

It is a neat categorisation and one that may well appeal to us. We understand information by putting things into categories. Our brains like to categorise information; to find pleasing patterns in what can otherwise appear as random and chaotic (Rosch, 1975). Yet if we resist the temptation to jump into one of the writer style boxes and reflect, we might see this from a different perspective. If I decide I am a 'builder writer', I could say that I have learned something about my own learning. I now know more about myself in relation to the task of writing than I did before, and so when I come to write again I can use this knowledge and approach my writing as a 'builder writer'. This bit of knowledge of myself has been added to my self-concept. However, this notion of a 'builder writer' was not something that came from me; it was something I read about, recognized myself in and adopted. The question I might want to ask myself then is, 'To what extent is putting myself in this category helping me to write better?' This can be a very difficult question to answer, because things that begin as helpful can become restricting and unhelpful over time. In addition, whilst we remain consciously aware of the fact that we have deliberately chosen to adopt the category of 'builder writer', it may be helpful for us. It may help us to see how we are writing. It may help us to avoid 'writers' block'; to section up work; to add another small brick to the wall; etc. At some point, though, and depending on the age at which we adopt the label, the notion of being a 'builder writer' will fall from our consciousness and reside at a subconscious level. It may still control how we approach writing tasks, but we may no longer have conscious control over changing it. We could substitute 'builder writer' knowledge for the much more ubiquitous and pernicious use of learning style categorisation in education.

The idea that learners can be categorised into particular types (e.g. visual, auditory, kinaesthetic) has taken hold in some schools despite there being no evidence for either the existence of specific learning styles from a neuro-scientific point of view, i.e. this is just not the way the brain works (Greenfield, 2000), nor is there any evidence that a learning style approach improves learning (Lilienfelf, Lynn, Ruscio and Beyerstein, 2010; Coffield, Moseley, Hall and Ecclestone, 2004). No doubt there are many adults, including a number of teachers, who were categorised as visual or auditory learners as children and continue to believe and behave as if this were the case. We noticed that at the start of the project in primary RE, many activities involved pupils in creative work such as making displays, using religious artefacts as models for creating individual pieces, colouring and collaging. We argue that a focus on creative activities in primary RE restricts children's view of religions, reducing them to a collection of artefacts, symbols and stories which can be re-created and manipulated and implies that RE as a subject is only about personal interpretation. Through education we not only build knowledge of the subject but also knowledge of ourselves as learners and thinkers in relation to that subject. Thus, the activities we provide for pupils in RE are crucial to the development of self-knowledge as well as subject-specific knowledge.

This knowledge built up over time, and with experience related to our own thinking or learning, is termed metacognitive knowledge.

Metacognitive knowledge

Metacognitive knowledge is one element of the broader concept of metacognition. In the next few sections I will build up to the full theory of metacognition, but having researched and worked with teachers on metacognition for the past 15 years, I am aware that sometimes the terminology used causes difficulty. Shying away from the use of technical terms, however, leads people to use such vague terms as 'thinking about thinking' or 'learning about learning'. These phrases do not do justice to the richness and variety of research and educational programmes which have flourished in the field of metacognition since the term was first used in the 1970s. It is important that we use the correct terms if we are to understand the research evidence. Metacognition is not the same as thinking skills, critical thinking, Bloom's (1956) taxonomy of higher order thinking, learning to learn or thinking together. Metacognition is a specific theory developed by developmental and cognitive psychologists to describe the reflective nature of the human (and some non-human animals) mind. It is a theory or set of ideas which requires empirical testing to provide evidence of its existence, its nature and its impact on learning.

The prefix 'meta' denotes something which comes after or goes beyond. The word 'cognition' refers to all mental processes by which we obtain knowledge. These are often categorised as reasoning, perceiving and intuiting. When we speak of something being 'meta', we are referring to something which goes beyond the normal state to a higher, more abstract level. In the case of knowledge, we can build up knowledge about a whole range of subjects throughout our lives. This knowledge is stored in long-term memory, and we can recall it when necessary. We also build knowledge about our own cognitive processes as we go through life, e.g. how we think or process information under different conditions; how reliable we believe our memory to be; how our own thinking differs from that of others or differs depending on the subject or task we are undertaking. This type of knowledge is described as metacognitive knowledge because it focuses not on what is in the world but on what is in our mind.

The most widely cited model of metacognitive knowledge is that created by Flavell (1979). In this model, metacognitive knowledge is broken down into three variables which interact together: person, task and strategy. The person variable focuses on what we know about ourselves in relation to our thinking processes; the task variable relates to our knowledge of the nature of the task and how this will impact on how we approach it. Task knowledge can include: the type of task; how the task is structured; whether all the information needed is present; and how similar the task is to other tasks. The strategy variable refers particularly to strategies which are aimed at our own information processing, e.g. strategies we might employ to help us to remember better; strategies which evaluate how well we know something; and strategies which focus on how we might approach a task and track our progress (planning, monitoring). These three variables interact to affect our learning. Whilst we may have gained some metacognitive knowledge of self, task and strategies, this does not mean that the knowledge we have is accurate, or that we always make use of it. It is quite possible to build up erroneous metacognitive knowledge about our thinking, e.g. that we are unable to tackle certain types of tasks or that we only think in one way (as a visual learner, for example). Just like other kinds of knowledge, our metacognitive knowledge may change over time, depending on our experiences. It can be inaccurate, redundant or we may forget what we know about our thinking processes. There is some dispute as to the extent to which metacognitive knowledge must be conscious, but most theorists agree that metacognitive knowledge should be at least available to consciousness (Baker, 1994), i.e. that we can retrieve the knowledge when prompted.

Do you make use of any metacognitive knowledge of self, task or strategy?

In addition to metacognitive knowledge, theories of metacognition also include two processes, which may not necessarily be conscious, but which run whilst we are doing a task. These are usually referred to as monitoring and control processes and are described as 'on-line metacognition', in contrast to metacognitive knowledge which is described as 'off-line metacognition'.

Monitoring and control

Monitoring and control processes are also termed regulation of cognition and include processes such as goal formation, attention control, planning, evaluating and revising. These processes are governed by executive functions in the frontal lobes of the brain (Luria, 1973), and there is considerable evidence of the importance of executive functions for enabling us to organize our thinking, adapt our behaviour to new situations, transfer knowledge from one situation to another and to self-regulate by inhibiting unhelpful behaviour. There is also some evidence that our higher levels of thinking such as those related to morality and ethical behaviour are dependent on our executive functions (Ardila, 2008). Studies of people with specific types of brain injury which affect the frontal lobes have found that following the injury, people have difficulty with abstract reasoning, decision making, organizing and planning (Jurado and Rosselli, 2007).

Nelson and Narens (1990) first described the processes of monitoring and control as functioning at different levels. They distinguish between self-monitoring, which refers to ongoing tracking of where you are in relation to a specific goal, and self-regulation, which is a more top-down process of employing the executive functions as control mechanisms. They describe an object level and a meta-level and liken the processes of monitoring and control to a telephone. The meta-level listens in to (or monitors) what is going on at the cognitive level. We may not be aware of this monitoring until something at the object level brings it to consciousness; most often this will be some kind of obstacle. When this happens, the control function sends a message back to the object level telling it what to do to overcome the problem and to remain on track. A good example of this is when we are reading. Fluent readers are not conscious of the skills they are using when reading; instead, the focus will be on comprehension, enjoyment or some specific goal such as finding particular information. However, if we come across an unfamiliar word or something unexpected in the text, the monitoring function, which has been operating (listening in) in the background will stop the flow of reading and identify the problem. The control function will then send an instruction back to the object level. This might be to 'ignore the word and continue reading' or to 'look the word up' or perhaps to 'note the word down to define later'. The control message will be dependent on the goal of reading. If we are reading for pleasure, it may be appropriate to skip the odd word, whereas if we are reading life-threatening information it will be important that we understand each word. The whole monitoring and control process can be so quick that we are barely aware of it, or it can be much slower and we may deliberate before taking action and continuing with the task. The monitoring and control processes interact with and draw on our metacognitive knowledge and can be influenced by context and social interaction; e.g. in collaborative group work, the group may act as a monitor and control on individual thinking and learning. Group work can both stimulate these processes and make individual monitoring and control processes visible.

The development of metacognition is the development of metacognitive knowledge and the development of monitoring and control processes. The next section considers why metacognition is important for learning.

Metacognition and learning

One of the most commonly asked questions at metacognition workshops is 'Will developing metacognition lead to better exam or test results?' The answer is that it is difficult to give a definitive answer. There are studies which have shown an increase in test scores following a metacognitive intervention in mathematics (Elliot, 1993; Mevarech and Fridkin, 2006); reading (Juliebö, Malicky and Norman, 1998); and science (Leopold and Leutner, 2015). In the RE-flect project, we reported gains in three of the schools we worked with (see Chapter 6). However, the majority of research studies on metacognition focus on the types of metacognitive behaviour pupils engage in under different conditions, or their own judgements and predictions about their own learning, rather than demonstrating impact on exam results. This may be because most metacognition research is carried out by psychologists rather than education practitioners and because it is very difficult to measure metacognition in a way which allows for correlation between metacognitive assessments and academic assessments. A further problem is that standard academic tests of attainment rarely take account of the metacognitive processes which led to the answer. The majority of short answer tests rely on pupils getting the correct answer. Longer and more complex tests tend to focus on understanding subject-specific content and/or assessing analytical and critical thinking, skills of writing such as creating an argument or sometimes creativity. Few tests focus on assessing metacognitive skills such as: task awareness, goal setting, selection of strategies, task management, outcome prediction, persistence, monitoring, revising and evaluating.

> How do you assess students in RE? Would it be possible to include assessment of metacognitive skills?

Pupils may be taught a rubric for completing a task. This is often the case with 'Thinking Skills' intervention programmes. These may include metacognitive skills; however, these programmes tend not to have a lasting effect because they fail to develop the self-knowledge required to regulate when and how the rubric should be used. A good example is the ubiquitous use of 'planning' as a strategy taught to primary school pupils who are learning to write; but many professional writers begin to write without a plan. It is perfectly possible to begin writing with an idea and for a plan to develop as the writing develops. Few children are taught to think about what kind of a writer they are and to match this metacognitive self-knowledge with the task, whilst also considering external factors such as time, audience, the importance of task and motivation. Thus, simply to teach children to plan when they have no understanding of why and when planning might be helpful and when not, hinders the development of children's own ability to regulate their thinking.

We might argue that it is not necessary to measure metacognition itself, but only its impact on learning in a specific subject area. Thus, if we run a metacognitive intervention programme we might expect to see our test results improve. Whilst there are some studies (highlighted earlier) which show increases in test results, it is often impossible to control for the other variables which may be influencing the positive result. There are a number of factors which can influence any education intervention, and not all researchers are clear about how these factors impinge on their research findings. Thus, research may overclaim to generalise findings from the specific site of the research to other classrooms. Dunlosky, Bottiroli and Hartwig (2009) listed the main factors which can influence research findings due to their variability, and these can be categorised into: (1) Teacher factors, e.g. teacher subject knowledge, teaching style, metacognitive orientation; (2) Learning environment, e.g. classroom layout, school location, access to resources; (3) Course materials, e.g. type of course, assessment practices, materials provided, subject domain and task. We could also add to these the socio-cultural elements of the classroom, including the way pupils interact with each other and with their teacher, and in RE we would also need to take account of pupils' own faith or non-faith backgrounds and experiences. It is thus very difficult to claim that any educational intervention 'works' in a more general sense, and it is important when reading research to be aware of the context of the research and the factors which have been accounted for and those which have not. No research can account for all the variables present in a complex learning environment, but that does not mean that we cannot learn things of value from research studies.

Whilst there is cumulative evidence that metacognitive intervention programmes have a positive effect on learning, it is also the case that other factors may be important. One factor which is closely linked to metacognition and is likely to be involved is motivation. There is a good deal of anecdotal evidence from our own study and from other studies that pupils enjoy metacognitive programmes because they see the relevance of learning about themselves as learners. In the RE-flect project, pupils came to see the relevance of understanding not just the content of different religion(s) and worldview(s) but how and why they are taught, as well as understanding how self-efficacy judgements and own beliefs can affect their learning and impact on outcomes. However, a previous study exploring primary pupils' beliefs about RE (Van der Zee, 2006) showed that whilst the pupils in the study were motivated to do well academically, they were not specifically motivated towards the curriculum context of the RE lessons. Children without a faith background may see less relevance in studying different faith positions. Indeed, in a project conducted by one of our colleagues, a pupil commented that there was no point in studying RE because 'I don't want to be a vicar' (Walshe, 2011). Yet one of the findings from the RE-flect project which was reported from both the teacher perspective (see Chapter 6) and from interviews with the children (see Chapter 7) was an increase in interest and enjoyment of the subject.

Creating a metacognitive learning environment

In creating a metacognitive learning environment, the RE-flect project takes a socio-cultural approach to facilitating metacognition. Surprisingly, this is not the norm for metacognitive interventions. Instead, the majority of classroom metacognitive programmes are based on teaching a set of strategies or steps which can be applied to specific problems. Programmes often use acronyms to remind pupils of the steps to be taken, e.g. IMPROVE (Mevarech and Fridkin, 2006), which is a metacognitive approach to mathematics. Teachers and pupils are encouraged to apply the rubric: I – introduce the new concepts; M – metacognitive questioning; P – practicing; R – reviewing; O – obtaining mastery; V – verification; E – enrichment and remedial. Similar approaches have been designed for other subject areas (although not RE), with strategies such as highlighting, mapping, visualising, using various types of graphic organizers and various rubrics. These approaches help pupils and teachers to focus on higher levels of thinking, but they do not mirror real-life learning and do not necessarily develop metacognitive self-knowledge. If we were to take these types of approaches to everything we want to learn, we would spend a lot of time on the steps and less time on understanding ourselves as learners. In schools, approaches such as these tend to be started with great enthusiasm but are often not maintained, and more importantly, we question whether the majority of pupils use these approaches outside of academic learning. There is nothing wrong with using strategies such as mind maps, graphic organizers and highlighters to manage data and focus thinking, but these methods do not go far enough to facilitate the development of metacognition for life-long learning. Instead we argue that fostering metacognition requires a change in the culture of classroom-based learning. This is a more holistic approach to creating the conditions for metacognition to develop, and so the RE-flect project adopts a socio-cultural approach to metacognition, which takes account of every aspect of the learning environment.

Learning environments include not only the physical layout of the learning space but also psycho-social features of the learning community, leadership and management and wider external societal and political pressures on the system. A great deal of research into learning environments focuses on exploring associations between the learning environment and pupil outcomes (see Fraser, 1998 for a review). Recent studies of learning environments also include the beliefs and attitudes of parents and, crucially, the expectations of teachers. We know from labelling theory that teachers' expectations of pupils can lead to a self-fulfilling prophecy with regard to learning outcomes (see the classic experiment by Rosenthal and Jacobson, 1968). However, in a metacognitive learning environment, learning outcomes or subject-specific attainment are not seen as only the result of the environment but as an element of the culture. Learning outcomes are multi-dimensional and include short-term meeting of task-specific goals but also changes in motivation, attitude and development of metacognition. These may be at both individual and group level. Crucial to developing a metacognitive learning environment is a focus on classroom interaction and relationships between teacher and pupil and pupil and pupil. This approach goes beyond introducing thinking skills-type strategy instruction; changing the curriculum or even changing how the learning environment is organized at a system level. Instead, creating a metacognitive learning environment requires a change in thinking as much for researchers into metacognition, who tend to focus on skills and individual development, as for school managers, teachers, parents and pupils who often focus on subject knowledge and attainment.

In the RE-flect project, we based our socio-cultural approach to facilitating metacognition on the work of Greg Thomas (2003). Having worked as a science educator in both Eastern and Western cultures, Greg has explored how changes to the learning environment are perceived by pupils. We adapted his work in science learning to learning in RE with a focus on developing the metacognition necessary to engage in dialogue with others of different faith and non-faith backgrounds. In order to create meaningful dialogue between faiths, a different kind of environment from one which is based on right and wrong answers is necessary. Johnston (1983) suggested that one of the first precepts is *'be attentive'* (p. 10); he makes the point that few of us truly listen to others; instead we are pre-occupied with getting our own point across, or with our own fears and anxieties. However, in being attentive, Johnston is referring to more than simply listening to the other. He suggests that being attentive also means listening to oneself, allowing ourselves to ask questions which come from the heart. The suggestion is that as we expose ourselves to other or non-faith traditions, we allow ourselves to be influenced by that tradition and thereby to perhaps expand our consciousness to see things differently. For young pupils, this may be the first time they have encountered religious dialogue which is not the same as their own (non-)religious background, and of course this may create anxiety, as it can for adults. But if we can teach children to listen properly and to ask genuine questions, we may enable them to develop the reflective self-awareness which is at the core of metacognitive knowledge. Johnston makes the point that this self-questioning leads to insight and to *'intelligence'*, but he goes on to say that insights are not knowledge until they are acted on by reason. The ability to use reason to integrate new and different knowledge into our consciousness is a goal of metacognitive development (Flavell, 1979). The other precepts necessary for inter-faith dialogue as suggested by Johnston are to *'be responsible'* – by this he means to recognise what is good in other faith and non-faith traditions – and to *'be committed'* to learning from dialogue with others. In the RE-flect project, we took the position that before encountering dialogue with others we should enable pupils to reflect on their own worldviews. It is not necessary to suspend our own views in order to enter into successful dialogue with others – this would be, in Johnston's terms, to *'lose our roots'* and find that we have nothing to share. In engaging with others of different and non-faith traditions, we are not suggesting compromising or watering down our own worldviews, nor to end up converting or committing to nothing; as Johnston says: 'This would be an aberration of what it means to be committed' (p. 12).

Our goal in the RE-flect project was to create learning environments in RE classrooms which would enable a commitment to dialogue with others through the development of metacognition. Learning environments are made up of a number of elements which we categorise under: physical space; tasks/activities; and relationships. In order to facilitate metacognition, we argue that educators need to take account of all three categories.

Physical space

We know that physical space affects people's ability to function, both physically and psychologically. Research into working environments has suggested that we need to think about three distinct areas of impact: (1) How much people feel a sense of belonging and ownership over the environment; (2) How satisfied people feel about the aesthetics of the space and its physical elements; (3) How the space affects people's performance (Vischer, 2008). However, Vischer's research relates to adult working environments, and the model has recently been re-conceptualised to fit school environments. The categories for schools are termed: Community; Well-being; and Working Successfully (Sheehan, 2015). These categories are relevant to creating a metacognitive learning environment and cohere with the RE-flect project's view of the importance of the physical space for developing metacognition.

One of the first things we asked teachers to do on the RE-flect project was to create three physical zones within their RE classrooms. These would consist of: a meta-thinking zone; a worldview zone; and a resources zone. Subsequent chapters will give details of each zone and how to create one in your classroom. A zone could be a table in the corner of a classroom; a window ledge; a shelf on a bookcase – the size of the zone was not important, and we worked in some tiny rural schools where space was definitely an issue. In addition, some of the RE teachers were not the main class teacher and felt at first that they could not change anything in the layout of the classroom. This highlights the issue of 'Who owns the classroom space?' We argue that if we are to develop learners who are metacognitive and self-regulating, then we need to facilitate a feeling of belonging and community within the physical space. This involves some flexibility over classroom space ownership.

> Who do you think owns the classroom space? Do you ever allow other adults and children to change the classroom spaces?

We found that although at first teachers thought it would be impossible to create three zones within their classrooms, either because of space or because they did not feel they could change another teacher's space, in fact all of our teachers did create the three zones.

We also created RE activities, which meant that classrooms sometimes had to be reorganised in terms of group work; to create space for building artwork; to facilitate interaction with external visitors; to make break-out groups for project work; or to facilitate individual writing and quiet time. The flexibility of the physical space can be seen as a metaphor for the flexibility in thinking required to develop metacognition. Thus, reflecting on the ownership of the physical space and how it can be used to support community and engender satisfaction and well-being is crucial to creating a metacognitive learning environment.

Tasks and activities

When Flavell (1979) first outlined his theory of metacognition, he gave us the conditions under which metacognitive experiences are most likely to happen. A metacognitive experience can be defined as a thought or feeling about an intellectual task. For instance, we might feel puzzled or confused about the nature of the task we are being asked to do; we might feel happy and motivated towards a task, or we might remember how badly we have done on similar tasks before and feel despondent. Any or all of these would constitute a metacognitive experience as long as we are conscious of what we are thinking and feeling. However, we rarely ask children to reflect on how they are thinking or feeling about a task. This may be because many of the tasks we ask children to undertake do not result in strong feelings which can be verbalised. Many of our children sleepwalk through school activities, displaying little or no emotion towards them. This is what Ellen Langer (1997) has termed 'mindless learning'. It is not that the activities in themselves are not beneficial for learning in a particular subject domain, but that the activities do not require higher levels of thinking which would develop metacognitive processes. But we can create metacognitive experiences for our learners in RE by following Flavell's prescription for learning activities, which suggests that *Complex tasks* are more likely to need metacognition than simple ones. *Open-ended* tasks require us to justify our answers. Tasks which require *Planning*, because planning is a metacognitive strategy – so get learners to plan, avoid planning for them, but make sure they understand why they are planning. Let learners decide what resources they need and how to get them. *Language* is very important – ask questions about thinking, talk about thinking, talk about knowledge, try to break out of your normal Q&A patterns which seek right answers and instead focus on thinking processes. *Collaboration* enables us to observe metacognition, and through dialogue with others we come to know more about ourselves. Collaboration can be part of a task; it does not have to be the whole task. Tasks should require *Decision-making* – when we have to make real decisions, we begin to reflect on how we are making them and hence on our thinking.

In any subject area, we need to focus on subject-specific content, and thus the activities we created for the RE-flect project cohere with a locally Agreed Syllabus for RE and include RE content on different faiths, including: Judaism, Buddhism, Islam, Christianity and Hinduism. You can find more about how the activities were created in Chapter 5, enabling you to create your own to fit your own local context.

Relationships

Crucial to the development of a metacognitive learning environment is the relationship between teacher and pupil and pupil and pupil. In the Physical Space category, we mentioned Community, and this is the term which best sums up the nature of the relationship between people in a metacognitive learning environment.

Some relationships are more conducive to fostering metacognition than other relationships. First, there needs to be some genuine and authentic relationship between teacher and pupil. By this we mean that respect is shown on both sides and that teachers reflect on the types of questions they ask and the language they use; e.g. Langer and colleagues showed that introducing subjects in a conditional manner, for example by using phrases such as 'could be', 'perhaps', 'from one perspective', rather than 'is', enabled pupils to use knowledge in new and creative ways. She has argued that focusing on where our attention is and making new distinctions between things can lead to greater openness and sensitivity to the environment and new information; create awareness of multiple perspectives; and enable new conceptions to form. These all seem pertinent to learning in RE, as of all the subjects; RE requires an openness to new and challenging knowledge as well as an awareness and sensitivity to how others might think and feel. So, whilst the first element in this relationship is to reflect on ourselves as teachers and educators and how we communicate with pupils, the second element is about genuine collaboration between pupils and between teacher and pupils.

Authentic collaboration is about working towards a common goal. Crucial to this is the development of good communication skills, particularly skills of listening. Making these visible through games enables the development of meta-communication skills, i.e. understanding that how we listen and engage with others affects progress towards the goal as well as affecting the group dynamics. It is through collaborating with others that we develop social metacognition. Social metacognition refers to our understanding of how others are thinking and feeling. It enables us to understand that people may think differently about something even though they are observing or reading about the same event. Social metacognition also enables us to put ourselves in the shoes of others and see the world through their eyes. In the RE-flect project we focused on both social metacognition through the 'Worldview Profiles' and through development of a learning community. We viewed community as a sense of belonging so that everyone must feel involved in the activities. Authentic project work can also foster this sense, particularly where the outcome of the problem is not known in advance. Other features of the RE-flect environment were roles and boundaries. This involves thinking about, and questioning, your own role as a teacher and where your boundaries are – is it possible to break through any boundaries in order to interact more authentically within the classroom and the community? Individual time was also an important factor in RE-flect – learners need time to themselves to reflect. We do not take the view that all learning comes through talk; instead, we believe that sometimes we need quietness and stillness to focus on ourselves, on the material presented to us and on conversations we have had. Thus, learning in RE is also about becoming self-aware. The final two features of our Relationships category of metacognitive learning environments were: Empowering others – we all make mistakes – mistakes are good because we learn from them, thus we need to create a safe psycho-social space in which mistakes are viewed positively; and Role models – we need to believe that it is important to develop metacognition if we are to succeed. We, therefore, need to develop our own metacognition as adults to act as role models to others.

To sum up, creating a metacognitive learning environment requires reflection on three areas: Physical Space; Tasks/Activities; and Relationships. Table 1.1 provides an overview of the elements in each category.

Creating a metacognitive learning environment should not be an arduous task. It is a myth to think that in order to develop and facilitate metacognition we need a whole-scale revolution in teaching. Instead, there are many small things you can do which fit within your own style of teaching that will impact on the development of metacognition. It is often the case that by engaging with small things first, we change the way we think about teaching and learning, and the revolution happens without our trying too hard. It is our belief that it is only through reflecting on and changing our own *thinking* about teaching and learning that we will foster metacognition in our pupils.

Table 1.1 Elements of a metacognitive learning environment

Physical space	Tasks/activities	Relationships
Meta-thinking zone	Complex tasks	Authentic
Worldview zone	Open-ended	Community and collaboration
Resources zone	Require planning	Roles and boundaries
Ownership of the space	Collaborative and individual	Individual development
Reflection/quiet space	Develop language	Empowering others
Flexibility of the space	Require decisions	Role models

The aim of a metacognitive learning environment is to: Create a safe psycho-social space where members of the community feel a sense of belonging; where it is OK to be wrong, to make mistakes; and where people are supported and empowered to learn together and to develop their individual self-awareness.

We will return to these elements in more detail in future chapters with examples of what you can do in your own classroom to achieve a metacognitive learning environment, not just in RE (although that will be the focus of many of our examples) but also in every other subject area.

Further reading

Ambridge, Ben. (2015) 10 myths about psychology: Debunked. Online. www.youtube.com/watch?v=ce31WjiVcY0 (accessed 7 June 2018).

Larkin, S. (2010) *Metacognition in Young Children*. Oxford, UK: Routledge.

Perfect, T.J. and Schwartz, B.L. (eds.). (2002) *Applied Metacognition*. Cambridge, UK: Cambridge University Press.

Meta-thinking zone 2

Creating a metacognitive learning environment involves changes both to the culture and the physical space of the classroom. We know that how space is used affects the type of activities and relationships that are fostered. If we seat pupils in rows all facing the same way, we give one impression of learning, which is that everyone should be doing the same thing at the same time, all eyes should be on the teacher, who will in turn dispense some form of knowledge which pupils will absorb. If on the other hand we seat pupils in groups, we give another impression of learning, which is that collaboration and co-operation are important and that we can learn from discussion with each other. We might argue that at different times both seating arrangements are valid, and teachers aware of these affordances will choose what is best for the specific learning objectives. Teachers also, of course, spend a great deal of time and effort in creating a welcoming and creative classroom space to facilitate learning. In the RE-flect project, we took the view that the physical space of the classroom is an important factor in facilitating the type of learning which leads to the development of metacognition. Thus, we asked teachers to create three zones in their classrooms. This chapter focuses on the meta-thinking zone. The aims of the meta-thinking zone are to develop a language of thinking; to encourage questioning, including self-questioning; to remind pupils to stop and reflect on their thinking; to build metacognitive knowledge; and to encourage regulation of thinking. We expect that by using the questions and prompts in the zone, pupils will also develop their listening skills as they learn to listen to the answers for the questions they pose to themselves and others.

In Chapter 1 we saw that metacognition can be divided up into metacognitive knowledge and regulation of cognition. We know that metacognitive knowledge, like any other kind of knowledge, develops with age and experience. We build knowledge about our own thinking as we experience more and different situations which force us to stop and reflect on our thinking. Regulation of cognition is different in that it can happen sub-consciously, e.g. when we correct errors without being aware of the monitoring and control processes that have enabled us to do that. Research has shown that monitoring and strategy choices can happen unconsciously (Reder and Schunn, 1996) and that we might not always be aware of our own feelings of knowing, yet we act on them (Diana and Reder, 2004). Most of the research about what metacognition is, how it differs from cognition and how and why it develops, what is commonly called 'foundational theory', is carried out by psychologists. However, as educationalists who draw on this psychological theory, our role is to focus on how we might aid the development of metacognition in our pupils and ensure that it has an educational impact.

In setting up a meta-thinking zone within our metacognitive learning environment, we focused particularly on the link between language and metacognition. Metacognitive processes are not wholly dependent on external language, e.g. we can observe a young child silently manipulate a jigsaw piece in order to make it fit in the correct space. Thus, demonstrating both monitoring – 'the piece doesn't fit' and control – 'I need to turn it around and try again'. Sometimes young children will vocalise their thinking as they problem-solve, but as they get older and are perhaps discouraged from 'speaking aloud', the voice is internalised. However, mainstream classroom learning is heavily language-based, and these days we go to great lengths to encourage pupils to engage in productive talk. In keeping with our theory of creating a metacognitive learning environment on the RE-flect project, the meta-thinking zone had a physical presence; was aimed at encouraging dialogue and inquiry; was flexible enough to be used for all RE-flect activities; and as we learned from the teachers on the project, was used across the curriculum. Whilst we always knew what we wanted this zone to do, we were at first unsure what to call it. After some deliberation, we settled on the term 'meta-thinking zone'. We wanted to indicate that the zone was there to encourage and facilitate a shift in thinking from the cognitive to the metacognitive level. The following sections describe in detail specific elements of this zone and how it was used in a RE-flect activity.

Focus on language

Understanding our own thinking requires us to develop a vocabulary to talk about thinking. Vygotsky's (1930–1934/1978) theory of learning focuses on the move from learning with help from a more knowledgeable other (a parent, care giver or sibling in the first instance) to more self-directed learning. Thus, the move is one from external dialogue with others to internal dialogue with ourselves. We internalise the voices which are initially external to us. Thus, there is a great deal of attention paid in early years education to talk. Much of the talk we engage in with infants is either social/emotional or knowledge-based in terms of naming things in the world or attempting to explain the world. However, by around the age of 3 years most children can distinguish between different 'mental state words' such as 'know', 'think', 'believe', 'imagine', 'guess', 'remember', but children often use these words inconsistently, and linguistic development focused on differentiating such terms continues throughout childhood. Lockl and Schneider (2006) have suggested that developing metacognitive knowledge aids in the comprehension of mental state words and developing an understanding of these words impacts on developing metacognitive knowledge. Thus, there is a two-way interaction between the development of the language of thinking and the development of metacognitive knowledge. This interaction is important to acknowledge because it demonstrates that we should not restrict children's access to these words until they are 'developmentally ready'; instead, by encouraging the use of these words we aid their metacognitive development. There is thus no right age to begin learning mental state words; instead, the more we use them, the better we support children's comprehension of them. In early years classrooms we can begin by focusing on the word 'think'. We might encourage pupils to think about what other people are thinking, or indeed if they are thinking at all. Some 4–5-year-olds will still maintain that someone sitting silently in a room is not thinking at all (Flavell, 2000). In encouraging pupils to think about what other people are thinking, we facilitate the development of a theory of mind, which is an understanding that different people think differently from each other even if they are experiencing a similar event (Carpendale and Chandler, 1996). Developing a theory of mind is part of social and emotional development and necessary for conflict resolution as well as part of cognitive development. This is clearly important for RE classrooms, as we want pupils to understand that others may have different views about life and faith from their own.

> Have you encouraged your pupils to use any mental state words? How might you enrich these conversations?

However, in some classrooms the use of the word 'think' becomes a routine devoid of meaning. Sometimes pupils are encouraged to start every sentence with 'I think', or when asked how they solved a problem, 'I thought about it' is accepted as an answer. In order to avoid this, we need to push pupils further and develop an understanding of the differences between mental state words, e.g. 'Do you think this?' or 'Do you know this?' We need to engage pupils in a conversation using mental state words, e.g. 'What is thinking hard?' 'How do we know when we are thinking hard about something?' 'What does thinking hard feel like?'

One of the important words for RE is 'believe'. We found that whilst all teachers used the words 'belief' and 'believe', at the beginning of the project no one had defined the word or differentiated it from other mental state words. Thus, we had many instances of lessons which included 'Hindus believe … ', 'Christians have different beliefs from Muslims', 'Some beliefs of Judaism are similar to those of Christianity', etc. In the RE-flect project, we decided it was necessary to take a step back and to focus on the word itself. Thus, we encouraged teachers to hold a conversation with their class around 'What we mean by belief', including questions such as 'Do we all believe the same thing?', 'Where do beliefs come from?', 'Can we believe different things at different times/ages?', 'How do you change your beliefs?' and 'What is the difference between believing and knowing?' Thus, before encountering the beliefs of others and before reflecting on their own beliefs, we developed some understanding of the word, and in doing so we began the mental process of shifting thinking from the cognitive to the metacognitive level. Other mental state words – 'know', 'guess', 'imagine' – can be used to provoke conversations, e.g. 'Do we know this or are we guessing?' Games can be used to differentiate between 'guessing', 'knowing' and 'imagining'. Art and role play are also useful here, e.g. drawing an animal we know exists and then drawing an imaginary animal. This can lead into a lesson on representation of different gods and symbolism inherent in religious imagery. Thus, we come to understand that something as simple as the placement of hands in a representation of the Lord Buddha has special and significant meaning. We can see how the facilitation of mental state words might lead to greater subject-specific knowledge and understanding.

Questioning

An important feature of the meta-thinking zone is the use of questions. In a metacognitive learning environment, we aim to move the focus of questioning from teacher–pupil to pupil–pupil and pupil–self. Research has shown that on average, pupils ask only 0.1 questions an hour in classes, and that most of these tend to be shallow factual questions, often related to task instruction (Graesser and Person, 1994), but many teachers are not aware of the discrepancy between the number of questions they ask and the number and type of questions asked by pupils. Questions have been categorised in different ways, for example, Graesser found that in normal conversation, four broad types of questions are used. Whilst some are aimed at gaining knowledge, others focus on monitoring the common ground between speakers. The other two categories are concerned with social actions and gaining attention. In any category, questions can be more or less genuine. In classrooms, the focus of questions is nearly always on addressing knowledge retrieval, and pupils are often given very little time to answer before the teacher moves on. This is obviously quite different from how we use questions in normal conversation, and one aspect of the creation of a metacognitive learning environment challenges us to develop more authentic relationships with pupils. Knowledge-based questions have their place in learning for testing comprehension and linking content between teaching sessions, but teachers can also model the rhetorical-type questions that facilitate metacognition. For instance, we might begin a question with 'I was wondering if … ' or 'I am asking myself why/how … ' or 'I had a question in my mind about … '. In this way, we can still focus on content knowledge but also demonstrate that everyone has questions, that there may be gaps or contradictions in task information, and that we all experience uncertainty, obstacles and confusion. Asking questions also demands that we listen to the answers, and this is a skill that many pupils need to learn in order to collaborate well on group tasks, so opportunities to practise listening are equally important.

There has been a good deal of research on how questions are answered. Cary and Reder (2002) have shown that whilst early views of question answering suggested that people try to retrieve information from memory first before trying any other strategy, in fact, people vary in the strategies they use. Thus, they found that whilst some people use a retrieval strategy, others use a plausibility strategy. This may account for some of the rather strange answers to questions posed to pupils, as they may be using a strategy which says if X was the answer to the last question, then it may well be the answer to this one. Asking children to rate their confidence in whether or not they know the answer may highlight this discrepancy. The mental state words of 'guess', 'know' and 'believe' could also be put to use if children give seemingly random answers, rather than simply saying that the answer itself is incorrect. It can be very useful and time-efficient to switch strategies, and Reder's work has shown that people select which strategy to use in answering questions based on intrinsic and extrinsic factors. Familiarity with the question and understanding the language used are intrinsic factors, whereas the context in which the question is asked and previous success with a particular strategy are deemed extrinsic factors. Cary and Reder's research (ibid) shows that when posed with a question, people first evaluate whether or not they are familiar with the question and the language used (intrinsic factors). If this evaluation leads to a strong feeling of knowing the answer, then a retrieval strategy is used first, whereas if the evaluation leads to a weak feeling of knowing, another strategy, such as plausibility, is used first. Thus, we switch between strategies depending not on the question asked but on our evaluation of our own internal state in relation to the question. The more complex the question, the more likely we are to rely on these feeling of knowing evaluations. The practical application of this for classrooms is that it may be useful to engage pupils in discussion about how they answer questions and to suggest that they may sometimes be using an 'educated guess', whilst at other times they may be confident that they know the answer. This can lead onto discussion around what to do when we are 'stuck' for an answer. Introducing pupils to strategies which they can use themselves will result in more self-regulated learning and the building of more positive metacognitive knowledge which, rather than resulting in 'I am no good at X', results in 'I don't think I know the answer to X, but I know I could find out'.

Setting up a meta-thinking zone

The meta-thinking zone is a physical part of the classroom, usually a wall display. It consists of a series of cards with single mental state words on them; a series of cards with questions and statements; and a selection of visual images, photographs and cartoons depicting people or animals thinking. Different features of the zone are focused on developing different aspects of metacognition: metacognitive knowledge; monitoring and control; and metacognitive experiences. The sections that follow give details of how this was done in the RE-flect project.

Metacognitive knowledge

Developing metacognitive knowledge is about developing awareness of our thinking processes and the conditions pertaining to them. We needed questions and statements which would facilitate metacognitive knowledge of self and tasks as well as metacognitive knowledge about the strategies which might be useful. Table 2.1 shows a selection of the statements and questions we used under these three areas of metacognitive knowledge; each of these was written on a separate card. Some teachers decided to colour-code the cards to represent the three areas: self, tasks and strategies.

There are other questions that can be asked in the category of metacognitive knowledge. When forming questions, think about the three sub-categories of Self, Task and Strategy, and focus on knowledge about thinking processes rather than knowledge that is task-specific.

Table 2.1 Metacognitive knowledge cards

Self	Task	Strategies
What do I already know that might help me?	Do I understand the task?	What strategies do I know that I could use?
What kind of thinking do I need?	What sort of question or task is this?	Do I need to plan?
Could I think about this differently?	Is this task like any other task I have done?	What do we need to do first?
What am I good at that is relevant here?	What is the goal?	What is the best way to reach the goal?
What strengths do my group have?	What resources are available?	How will I find what I need to know?
How should the roles be allocated to make best use of my group's strengths?	What do we need to focus on?	What do I know about group work that might help us?
What do I believe?	What is the deadline?	How will I know when I have done enough?

A question such as 'What is the goal?' is general, aimed at developing our understanding that tasks have goals, and whilst these will be different, it is a good idea to think about what the goal is before we begin the task. Thus, we begin to develop knowledge of different task goals which we can later draw on as we compare new tasks with those we have already done. Similarly, questions such as 'Is this task like any other task I have done?' and 'What is the best way to reach the goal?' force us to first compare the task with others and look for common features and then to search our knowledge of strategies we might have used successfully in the past to employ in the new situation. Questions in the 'Self' category are aimed at deepening our knowledge of our own unique thinking processes, and whilst these may differ depending on the task in front of us, we may over time become aware of some common features which we can use to our advantage. The goal in developing metacognitive knowledge is so that we can transfer the knowledge we have about learning to any task/situation, whether this is within the classroom or in life more generally. The three-part structure of metacognitive knowledge is a theory which helps us to distinguish between the different aspects and thereby enables us to target the different knowledge categories. However, in reality we move quickly between these categories, and categories overlap, e.g. it is debatable whether the question 'Do I understand the task?' is a Self or Task question, as it overlaps the two categories. In the RE-flect project, teachers did not categorize the questions on their displays with word labels; instead, they used a selection of questions from each category. These could be changed and refreshed from time to time.

Metacognitive monitoring and control

As explained in Chapter 1, metacognitive monitoring and control processes are the ongoing, often sub-conscious processes which track our thinking and enable us to correct errors; to change course and to stop and reflect more deeply, drawing on our metacognitive

Table 2.2 Monitoring and control cards

Individual level	Group level
Have I chosen the right strategy for this task?	How is my group working together?
How well is it going?	Have we made any mistakes?
What will I do next?	Do we have a plan for how we will work together?
Am I listening to others?	How close are we to the goal?
How would I rate my thinking/learning in this lesson?	Do we need to stop and reflect on where we are?
Could I have done anything differently?	What did we do well?
	What do we need to improve?

knowledge. In creating questions for the meta-thinking zone, we focused on both individual monitoring and control processes and those at group level. All the RE-flect activities involved some form of group work, either for the whole or for part of a lesson. This is in line with our inquiry-based approach to RE as outlined in the Introduction.

We are not usually aware of when we are monitoring and controlling our thinking, so by reminding children to reflect, we bring these processes to consciousness. Thus, we learn more about ourselves and our resilience when things do not go to plan (see Table 2.2).

Metacognitive experiences

Learning is an emotional activity, and metacognitive experiences happen when we become aware of our emotional response to a learning situation. There are different types of feelings described in theories of metacognition, e.g. feeling of knowing (FOK); this is also linked to what are called tip of the tongue experiences (TOT), which we have all experienced when trying to recall things from memory. We might also experience something as familiar (FOF) or as difficult (FOD), and we might then feel confident (FOC). We can make use of these feelings to help us to judge and evaluate our own progress. These processes are termed judgements of learning (JOLs), and the more accurate our judgements, the better we are likely to be at self-regulating our learning. As Eflikides (2002) has pointed out, as well as providing information about cognitive processes (e.g. that we can remember something), these judgements also have an emotional character. We experience the feelings of puzzlement, confusion, difficulty or pleasantness, ease and satisfaction. In RE, as we deal with sensitive and highly personal views, pupils may feel conflicted by encountering a different view of the world from the one espoused by their parents and family. How we perceive these feelings and act upon on them is personal and individual. In order to develop more self-regulatory learning behaviour, we need to be able to manage the emotional side of learning as much as the cognitive side. It is therefore important to provide pupils with opportunities for metacognitive experiences. The conditions under which they are most likely to occur as described by Flavell (1979) were outlined in Chapter 1. Table 2.3 gives a selection of the questions we used to enable pupils to reflect on their feelings.

It may take a while for pupils to feel confident about expressing their feelings about a task, especially if those feelings are negative. By creating a meta-thinking zone with some of these statements, we remind everyone that it is valid to reflect on our feelings and that our feelings

Table 2.3 Metacognitive experience cards

Individual level	Group level
How do I feel about this task?	How confident is the group that we can complete the task?
Is it easy or difficult?	How can we make this a happy group?
Am I interested in this topic?	How will we include everyone?
How might learning this affect me?	How is this task making everyone feel?
What colour best represents my feelings?	How satisfied are we with what we have done?

about a task change prospectively during the task and retrospectively after we have completed it. Some of the questions in this series can be used at the end of a lesson as an evaluation, but it is important that this is not the only time the meta-thinking zone is referred to.

Many practitioners use questions similar to those in the meta-thinking zone in their teaching, but without the consistency and coherence necessary to develop metacognition.

Different schools on the RE-flect project configured their meta-thinking zones differently. It is important that the zone includes mental state words as well as some of the questions from the different series.

In the next section, we show how the meta-thinking zone can be used in different RE-flect activities, drawing on data from the project schools.

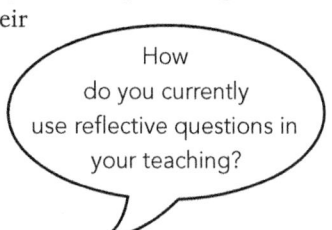

How do you currently use reflective questions in your teaching?

Using the meta-thinking zone in RE

As outlined earlier, we were concerned to focus attention on 'belief' before encountering different beliefs. Thus, one of the first lessons used the meta-thinking zone directly. Before this lesson, teachers had already introduced the pupils to the three zones and encouraged them to become involved in the creation of the displays. The aim was two-fold: first, this would encourage pupils to take an active part in how the classroom environment was configured; second, this would signal a move to an RE pedagogy which would engage pupils in dialogue about RE aims, content and ways of learning. The lesson on 'belief' and 'believe' also made use of the 'Worldview Profiles' (see Chapter 3) as pupils wrote about their beliefs. Teachers could return to this lesson later in the term and ask pupils to reflect on whether or not there had been any change in their beliefs during that time.

Lesson 1

Learning objectives: Reflect on important possessions, people, values, beliefs and places.

1. Starter activity: Play a song such as 'I Believe' by Frankie Laine.
2. Whole class discussion: What do you think this song is about? How do you know?
3. Introduce the theme of the lesson(s) – and write 'belief' on the board.
4. I believe ... : Pupils individually create a set of 'I believe ... ' cards. They then sort these into order, putting the ones they feel are most important to them at the top.

At this point, they can be asked to complete a section of their 'Worldview Profile' on 'All about me' (see Chapter 3). Pupils are asked to choose one of the beliefs that they are happy to talk about with other people. The teacher draws on the meta-thinking zone (individual metacognitive experience series) to pause the class and ask them to reflect for a moment on why they are happy to talk about that particular belief with others but perhaps not so happy to talk about another belief.

5. We believe … small group task: Each member of the group puts their belief card on the table and explains why they hold that belief. As a group, they must decide which of the cards they all agree with and place them on the table. If there is more than one card, they should choose the one that they think is most important to them all. Each group presents their group belief card to the rest of the class, explaining why they hold that belief.
6. Whole class discussion: Teacher leads the discussion, beginning with whether there is any belief amongst those presented which they think everyone in the class agrees with. If there is, put this belief on the board: 'We believe … '. If not, either put the most popular on the board or put up each group's belief card.
7. What does it mean to 'believe'? Whole class discussion: Refer to the belief statement(s) on the board, and drawing on the meta-thinking zone questions, discuss the nature of belief, e.g. what is the difference between saying 'we know … ' and 'we believe … '?

   When this lesson took place in the project, it emerged that pupils thought that the difference between the two terms was that if we know something, we can prove that it is true. If we believe something, we might not be able to prove it is true.
8. Small group task: The group task is to decide whether the whole class believes a statement is 'true'. For example, if the whole class believes that 'everyone is equal', the task is to decide if it is true that indeed everyone is equal and to discuss how they know this, i.e. What is the evidence? Where does the evidence come from? And how reliable is it?
9. Whole group discussion: Ask each group to state whether or not they thought the belief statement was true and to explain why/why not? Does it matter if you cannot prove a belief to be true? Why/why not?
10. Small group task: Invite each pupil to approach the meta-thinking zone and take a card from the monitoring and control group level cards. Each pupil has to read out and answer in their groups. As well as the questions in Table 2.2, teachers also used these questions:
    Q: How did your group overcome disagreements?
    Q: What part of your discussion made you think really hard?
    Q: Did you change your mind during your group discussion? Why/why not?
    Q: What have you learnt as a result of this group task and why?

During the project, we also asked teachers to reflect at the end of each lesson on where they would go next and to evaluate the lesson in their reflective diaries (see Chapter 7).

Whilst this lesson relates directly to developing metacognitive knowledge of self and others, the lesson that follows focuses much more on RE content, whilst still making use of the meta-thinking zone.

Lesson 2

Prior to this lesson, teachers were asked to begin to create a three-part wall display on Buddhism. The wall display would illustrate and summarise pupils' answers to the following three questions:

Part 1: What do I already know about Buddhism?
Part 2: What questions do I still have about Buddhism?
Part 3: When I was learning about Buddhism, what made me think very hard?
Parts 1 and 2 should be completed before the following lesson is taught. Part 3 should be completed after the unit of work on Buddhism.

This lesson involves groups moving around the classroom to explore a topic in five different ways. Thus, the classroom needs to be organised into five stations.
    Learning objective: To understand why images of the Buddha are important for Buddhists
    Station 1: Reflection on the nature of the task. Exactly what pupils on this table will discuss will depend at which point in the lesson they are at this station. Cards from the meta-thinking zone, Task and Experience series can be used or adapted, e.g.:

Q: What is the key question you are trying to find out the answer to?
Q: What sort of question is it?
Q: How might the answer to this question affect you?
Q: What do you already know that will help you to answer this question?
Q: What other information do you need to be able to answer this question?
Q: How might you go about finding this information?

Station 2: The focus here is on pupils drawing on their personal experiences to reflect on the idea of complete understanding. Art materials are provided with the following instructions: Use the art materials on the table to illustrate:

A big thing in life that you understand.
A big thing in life that you don't understand.
How it would feel if you understood everything.
If you understood everything, would you think differently? Feel differently? Act differently?

Station 3: Pupils encounter an image of the Buddha and explore why this image is important for Buddhists.
    Look carefully at the image of the Buddha on your table.

Q: What do you notice about this image?
Q: What words would you use to describe this image?
Q: How does this image make you feel?
A video clip of a Buddhist temple was played, and pupils discussed the following questions:

36 Meta-thinking zone

Q: Why does the Buddha look the way he does in this image?
Q: Why do you think this image of the meditating Buddha is important for Buddhists?
Q: How do you think Buddhists might use this image of the Buddha to remind them of who they can be?

Station 4: Pupils reflect on the Buddhist concept of enlightenment:

Q: Why do Buddhists believe that the Buddha was enlightened?
Q: How did the Buddha think differently? Feel differently? Act differently?
Q: What do you think it means to be enlightened?
Q: What qualities do you think an enlightened person would have?
Q: Would an enlightened person think differently? Feel differently? Act differently?
Q: What do you think a person would have to do to become enlightened?
Q: How would you know if a person was enlightened?
Q: If you were able to talk to a Buddha (enlightened person), what would you say? What would you ask?

Station 5: Reflection on learning: Exactly what pupils on this table will discuss will depend upon which point in the lesson they are at. Questions from all areas of the meta-thinking zone may be appropriate here, including:

Q: What have you learnt so far about this topic (either during or before this lesson)?
Q: What aspects of this topic interest you the most and why?
Q: What aspects of this topic do think you understand best?
Q: How could you prove to someone else that you understand those aspects?
Q: What aspects of this topic puzzle you and why?
Q: What would help you to understand those aspects better and why?

Plenary (whole class discussion):
  Assessment of learning: The focus here was on making the connection between the content of the lesson and learning about the self in relation to that content. Questions included:

Q: What is the answer to the key question?
Q: How do you know?
Q: How has the answer to this question affected you?
Q: What questions do you still have about this topic?

Reflection on learning:

Q: What was it like starting the lesson at Station 1/Station 2/Station 3/Station 4/Station 5?
Q: Do you think the lesson would have felt different for you if you had started at a different table?
Q: Would you have learnt more or less? Why?
Q: Would your learning have felt different? Why/why not?

Practical considerations

Teachers selected the most appropriate questions to use depending on the age group of the pupils and where in the sequence of RE-flect activities this lesson came. One of the RE-flect practitioners devised a traffic light scheme for evaluating and reflecting on learning, involving cards with one of the meta-thinking zone questions, e.g. 'How has your group worked today?' Green – very good, very well, very hard. Orange – quite good, quite well, quite hard. Red – not good, not well, not hard. Crucially, the pupils had to agree on which card to select and also to 'make sure you can explain why you have selected that colour if you are asked'. Without this need to explain, we would not be facilitating the development of metacognition but simply scoring the work done.

The RE-flect activities were designed to fit in with the locally Agreed Syllabus for RE, but of course, different schools had their own year plans for RE, so the use of activities such as those mentioned earlier were used at different times of the year by different schools. A further consideration was for schools to consider the local community and external factors. Thus, for one school the Buddhist activity fell during a local art/faith initiative, so more art-based work was produced during the lesson. Whilst we encouraged the use of the meta-thinking zone throughout the lesson, it was also important to achieve a balance between task-based work and the deliberate shift in thinking to the meta-level. It is important to acknowledge that metacognition is facilitated throughout the task, whether or not this is directly observable. In using the meta-thinking zone, we were aiming to make the inner voice speak aloud in order to share this with others, to act as a model for others and to encourage constructive development of the individual metacognitive voice. The meta-thinking zone aims to aid the transfer of learning from the specific context to other areas. The next section focuses on the nature of transfer and why it is so difficult to achieve.

Do you think you will be able to set up a meta-thinking zone in your classroom?

Transfer

Transfer is the ability to use understanding and knowledge constructed during one activity and transfer that understanding and knowledge to other similar tasks. In order to do this, we need to abstract some general principles from the first task and then apply these to the new situation. This seems straightforward, but in reality, it is the most difficult aspect of learning. Researchers tend to identify two types of transfer: near transfer, which refers to transferring knowledge, understanding and skills to other problems which are very similar to the initial problem either in content or in structure. Far transfer, on the other hand, refers to transferring knowledge, understanding and skills to problems which are not similar in structure and which may be more complex and open-ended than the original task. Hatano and Inagaki (1992) make a distinction between 'routine experts' and 'adaptive experts'.

Routine experts are able to apply a set of procedures or principles to a problem and come to a suitable or correct solution. Adaptive experts, however, have knowledge and understanding of the subject area which allows them to imagine different scenarios, to make predictions and thereby to transfer their learning to new contexts. One of their studies involved nursery aged children learning to care for goldfish. They argue that the children developed conceptual knowledge about the need to both feed and care for the environment the fish lived in. The children were then able to transfer this knowledge to caring for other animals.

It is thus important to include questions related to transfer both during and at the end of any RE-flect lesson, e.g. discuss any rules that were employed in a particular task; reflect on how they came to an agreement or to new understanding; and ask how we might use what we have learned today in other contexts. The ability to transfer learning across contexts marks the development of expertise in a subject and is clearly linked to self-regulated learning. Once we are able to analyse how we learned something and to discern the features of the task we are given, we are able to use this knowledge to learn things for ourselves.

Further reading

Mitchell, P. and Riggs, K.J. (eds.). (2000) *Children's Reasoning and the Mind*. Hove, UK: Psychology Press.
Robson, S. and Flannery Quinn, S. (eds.). (2015) *The Routledge International Handbook of Young Children's Thinking and Understanding*. Abingdon, UK: Routledge.
Shayer, M. and Adey, P. (eds.). (2002) *Learning Intelligence*. Buckingham, UK: Open University Press.

Teacher voice 1
Creating a meta-thinking zone in my RE classroom (Helen)

Space in the classroom is always at a premium, with display space particularly valuable. As a PPA cover teacher, to take some of this space took quite a bit of negotiation but was definitely worth the effort.

The meta-thinking zone through RE was built up over a term and remained a working feature of the classroom. I came to realise that the children throughout the school were being given opportunities to reflect on their learning but weren't being shown how this could happen or what it could look like. Traffic light assessment with a learning comment was the expected method, but the children didn't know what the learning comment could look like to give it value.

Through RE lessons, we used this lack of direction as a starting point. We used the prompts (from our meta-thinking zone display) to reflect on aspects of the lesson like 'How is my group working?' These were discussed first with the whole group. We explored what was needed from the group for successful and productive work and what it might look like. We put it into practice and then reflected at the end, asking 'How do we know our group worked well together?' This reflection could be through a discussion, wipe board comments or sticky notes – these added to the interactive meta-thinking zone wall display, too. We revisited this approach to group work a number of times. It was useful from a teaching point of view to see how the expectations of group work were raised and, as a teacher, how the phrasing of questions was important for it to be successful.

Moving on to developing metacognition as part of the curriculum, the introductory lesson on Hinduism with Year 5s worked especially well. Using the prompts: what do I – know, think, remember, guess and believe, group discussions were particularly rich, with the children spending a lot of time distinguishing between the criteria, and raised many questions – If I remember something, do I therefore know it? If I guess something, is it because I remember something about it? The session proved to be a great means to find a starting point to inform future learning. It also provided a good opportunity to evaluate group work.

Time was given to other reflective questioning in the same way and, over time, we added a bit more each lesson to our thinking toolbox. The regular class teacher commented that the self-reflection at the end of each of her lessons was moving away from bland statements and was increasingly more informative and reflective. Rather than simple statements like 'I found this tricky' or 'This was easy', the children went on to add further explanations. This added to the bigger picture of each child's understanding. For example, 'I found this tricky and I think I need to ask for help sooner', or 'I found the answers in a different way to how you showed us'.

Building up the meta-thinking zone over time paved the way for considering big questions about beliefs. It enabled the children to articulate their thoughts and views by questioning why they know something and what it means to them. Often, these beliefs had been handed to them through family beliefs or expectations and they had never been explored. This was often a very personal area, and reflective journals were a successful way to explore this.

Metacognition didn't just happen: it's a skill process that took time to build but was worth investing in. Primarily, the focus in school has been in RE, but its effect has rippled through other aspects of school life, too.

The worldview zone   3

The worldview zone within RE-flect project classrooms was designed to enable pupils to recognise, reflect on, understand and articulate their own worldviews. Alongside the presentation of thought-provoking questions and statements (e.g. posters and other types of display), the principal technique for stimulating pupils to reflect on their own individual worldviews was the use of what we called 'Worldview Profiles'.

Background

Pupils bring to their learning their own assumptions about the world, and these assumptions shape what they learn. The assumptions might include the beliefs, values, perceptions, principles and frameworks by which they see, make sense of and give coherence to the world and to their own experience and behaviour (Commission on Religious Education, 2018). These assumptions might encompass, for example, views about the nature of reality, the meaning and purpose of human life and what constitutes a good life, as well as answers to questions of identity, belonging, commitment, behaviour and practice. Even though any hypernym is open to contestation, we use the catch-all term 'worldview' in its broadest sense to describe these different approaches to life. Accordingly, we can say that each pupil has their own evolving personal worldview, which may or may not be clear, coherent and/or consistent with the worldviews of others. It may be more or less systematic and more or less consciously held. Furthermore, it may or may not make explicit reference to an 'institutional worldview', that is, a perspective informed by membership of, and/or participation in, a (non-)religious institution or community, such as Christianity, Islam, Buddhism, Humanism or Confucianism (Commission on Religious Education, 2018).

What is important is that each pupil's worldview is recognised; that each pupil is respected regardless of the worldview they hold; and that conversations occurring within RE are inclusive of pupils of all religious and non-religious persuasions. The personal evaluations that pupils make of what they learn in RE might pertain to its truth, beauty, goodness, relevance, significance and so forth. Pupils may not be aware that they are making such evaluations influenced by their assumptions. They may not be aware that these evaluations and assumptions are integral to the learning experience, affecting both their ability and motivation to learn, for example. As Stephen Pett has argued,

> [in seeking to help pupils recognise their own perspectives] we are not trying to inculcate any religious or non-religious beliefs into pupils; we are helping them to realise that they look at the world through lenses of their experience too: they stand somewhere in relation to the material they are studying. We want them to be aware of where they stand in relation to being complex insiders/outsiders, to be aware that they have a position and that it affects how they encounter and respond to the content of RE.
>
> (Pett, 2018, p. 54)

We believe RE should help each pupil to bring their own personal worldview to consciousness, as well as enable them to articulate and monitor their worldview regularly. Thereby, they will better understand their own interpretation of, and engagement with, RE curriculum content, and they will be able to engage more deeply and in more genuine dialogue with others. For these reasons, RE should provide pupils with opportunities for personal evaluation and self-reflection (i.e. focusing on the subjectivity of the learner and why this matters), so that they gain knowledge of their own worldview, and knowledge of how their worldview influences, and is influenced by, their learning about religion(s) and worldview(s). Thus, the exploration of beliefs and values in RE is not limited to the exploration of other people's beliefs and values, but also of the pupils' own.

In our view, the purpose should not be to promote a particular form of personal, human, spiritual, moral, social or cultural development (for example based on a notion of implicit religion or innate spirituality). Neither should it be to encourage pupils to identify so-called 'signals of transcendence' in their own lives by studying them in depth. This has sometimes been promoted by making explicit links between purported 'common human experiences' (e.g. awe, celebration, passage of time, a quest for meaning, purpose and value) and 'religious experiences' (e.g. rituals, festivals, rites of passage, beliefs about God and the world). Instead, we believe the purpose should be to promote pupils' metacognitive knowledge about their own developing worldviews because personal reflection and reflexivity are intrinsic parts of what it means to undertake an academic study of religion(s) and worldview(s).

> Can you think of an occasion when your own worldview affected your motivation or ability to learn?

In the Introduction it was stated that the purpose of RE is to induct pupils into the ongoing dialogues of the communities of academic inquiry concerned with the study of religion(s) and worldview(s), for example, through theological, religious and related studies. Those who contribute to these dialogues often do so by reflecting upon their philosophical and theoretical positioning as researchers and being reflexive about the impact this positioning has upon their studies (e.g. in terms of influencing the selection of research questions, methodologies and methods and interpretative and analytical frameworks). It is widely accepted, particularly in the humanities, arts and social sciences, that different researchers will approach their research in different ways and from different perspectives, leading to the development of different understandings that are potentially equally valid and reliable. This reflects a general understanding that the standpoint of individuals (i.e. the point from which they see and understand the world) is shaped by their experiences, and also shapes, for example, what theories and concepts they deem credible, relevant and significant. If RE is conceptualised as a journey in which pupils move from peripheral to full participation in the ongoing dialogues of the communities of academic inquiry concerned with the study of religion(s) and worldview(s), then as part of that journey they need to develop ever greater critical reflexive awareness of themselves as learners, meaning-makers and knowledge-producers.

Challenging existing theory, policy and practice

Other researchers, to whom we are indebted for their inspiration, have also advocated the need for pupils to recognise, reflect on, understand and articulate their own personal worldviews, albeit with slightly different rationales to each other and to us. They include Michael Grimmitt (1987), Robert Jackson (1997), Andrew Wright (2000) and Clive and Jane Erricker (see, for example, Erricker, Sullivan, Erricker, Logan and Ota, 1994). Grimmitt's distinction between (1) *learning about* religion(s) (an impersonal and public form of understanding) and (2) *learning from* religion(s) (an impersonal evaluation of what pupils have learned about, but also a personal evaluation of their own subjectivity gained through enhanced self-knowledge) influenced how RE policy and curriculum documentation conceptualised the reflexive development of children's worldviews for decades (see Qualifications and Curriculum Authority [QCA], 2000 and 2004). In the main, however, pupils have been required to reflect on their worldviews in the light of their learning about religion(s) but not required to reflect on their learning about religion(s) in the light of their personal worldviews. Unfortunately, the phrase *learning from religion* as literally understood implies a unidirectional linear movement – from object of study to the subjective learner – rather than a two-way interactive process. Principled objections to this inference, as well as the difficulties experienced by teachers in understanding the term *learning from religion* (Teece, 2010), are perhaps two reasons it has more recently fallen out of favour.

Requiring pupils to express their personal beliefs, values and practices in relation to specific religious and non-religious worldviews may inhibit the ability of pupils from other religious and non-religious persuasions to articulate and develop their own worldviews, using their own concepts, theories and narratives. What kind of religious, spiritual and/or worldview literacy are we promoting if we only allow pupils to express themselves with reference to the language of others? Multi-faith RE should seek to produce polyglots who possess knowledge of many religious and non-religious languages but who nevertheless have an opportunity to develop their 'mother-tongue', reflecting upon it in relation to the voices of others but also in isolation from them.

The primary reason why profound existential, epistemological, ethical and other such questions should be raised in non-denominational RE in schools without a religious affiliation is not because RE is deemed uniquely placed as a curriculum subject to provide answers to 'ultimate questions' but because pupils' answers will affect and be affected by their engagement with the subject matter. If pupils are not cognisant of this fact, then they will be incapable of monitoring and regulating their learning, and they will act in response to the curriculum content in ways determined by subconscious beliefs and values. If there is a dissonance between the object of study and the personal worldview of the subjective learner, then that should be made explicit, explored and explained, so as to enrich the learning experience and increase the extent to which the learner is in control of the learning process. An individual's ability to recognise their own ontological, epistemological and ethical position as a position – therefore bounded and limited – has implications for their capacity to enter into genuine dialogue with those who hold other positions. Thus, we need to develop pupils' critical self-awareness of their own beliefs, values and assumptions as learners in RE and focus on their thinking about, and responses to, what they are learning. We also need to develop techniques for assessing whether pupils are making progress in these regards.

The need for a new approach

At the start of the century, *Religious Education: Non-statutory Guidance on RE* (QCA, 2000) was right to call upon teachers to create safe and positive learning environments and to plan activities to elicit pupils' responses to learning about religion(s) in an open and respectful manner in which personal conclusions can be actively drawn and articulated. There have been too few attempts to devise pedagogical principles and practices to support pupils – in a systematic and coherent fashion – to explore, develop and communicate their personal worldviews. Existing methods often resulted in isolated, sporadic and ad hoc opportunities which militated against pupils being able to analyse and synthesise their worldviews in an in-depth, continuous and methodical manner. Furthermore, the aims of such techniques were often incoherent, subconscious or covert.

For these reasons, on the RE-flect project we endeavoured to make explicit and clear the aims, methods and content of learning activities orientated around pupils gaining knowledge of their own personal worldviews and of how these influence, and are influenced by, their learning about religion(s) and worldview(s). The focus of such metacognitive self-exploration was to enhance the self-awareness, autonomy and self-regulatory capability of the learner. Neutrality in the study of religion(s) and worldview(s) is impossible, whether in school RE or university-based theological, religious and related studies, but knowledge of one's own partiality and the partiality of others is not. Reflection and reflexivity are pre-requisites for such self-knowledge and self-regulation. It enables pupils to feel confident and competent participating in learning experiences which might challenge or change their frames of reference, habits of mind and points of view.

Worldview education and framework

In terms of classroom practice, the approach we advocated on the RE-flect project was influenced by the work of John Valk on 'worldview education'. Valk (2009) defines 'worldviews' as comprehensive and integrative frameworks by which we understand ourselves, others and the world in which we live. For him, they are the lenses that inform our perceptions of reality and in turn form our perceptions of reality; but as much as they are visions of life, they are also ways of life. This is an important acknowledgement because worldviews can encompass many and varied aspects of human life, for example, influencing one's understanding, moral decisions, relationships and modes of expression (Commission on Religious Education, 2018, p. 72). They can refer to propositional beliefs but can also have emotional, affiliative and behavioural dimensions.

Valk (2009b) hopes that by using the term 'worldview' rather than 'religion', he is encompassing 'the wide variety of beliefs and values, religious or otherwise, that determine thoughts and actions' (p. 12). In so doing, he hopes to repudiate 'the popular myth that those who admit to no religious affiliation thereby embrace no faith', when actually they embrace worldviews such as secularism, capitalism, humanism and atheism (p. 5). To assist the conceptualization of the process by which pupils reflect upon and examine the religious and secular worldviews of others (knowing others), and thereby come to a greater understanding of themselves (knowing the self) (Valk, 2009a), Valk has developed an inter-disciplinary framework that draws upon a number of previous worldview definitions, descriptions or models (Valk, 2010). These encompass: (1) responses to life's larger concerns or questions; (2) questions of ultimate meaning and penultimate concerns about ordinary life and immediate personal concerns; (3) experiential, mythic, doctrinal, ethical, ritual and social dimensions; and (4) stories or narratives that define human reality (Valk, 2009b).

In the context of the RE-flect project, we adopted Valk's worldview framework (as represented in the first 2 columns of Tables 3.1–3.5) and translated its components into questions

Table 3.1 Worldview Question Framework (WQF) 1

Framework 1	Components	Questions
Personal Identity	Ethnicity, nationality, gender, orientation	How would you describe yourself?
	Family, community: rural, urban, religious/spiritual	How would you describe your home life?
	Socio-economic status: lower, middle, higher[1]	How would you describe your friends? How far do you share the same beliefs? What ideas do you agree and disagree with?
	Education: levels, schools	How would you describe your school?
	Abilities, disabilities: physical, intellectual, artistic, emotional	What do you like doing at school and at home? What are you good at? What do you dislike doing? What are you not so good at?

[1] The project team decided that socio-economic status was not an appropriate topic about which to ask pupils questions. Instead, we decided to ask a question about friendship, which is often an important issue for children.

Table 3.2 WQF 2

Framework 2	Components	Questions
Ultimate and Existential Questions	Meaning/purpose of life	Do you think there is a meaning and purpose to life? Can you explain your answer?
	Responsibility/obligations	Do you think people have responsibilities or duties to fulfil? Can you explain your answer?
	Discerning right/wrong	What do you think is right and wrong? What do you think is good and bad behaviour?
	Righting our wrongs	What do you think should happen to people who do wrong or behave badly?
	Greater force or power	Do you think there is a God or a higher being, force or power? How would you describe this?
	Life after this life	Do you think there is life after death? Can you explain your answer? If you do, can you describe what it would be like?

Table 3.3 WQF 3

Framework 3	Components	Questions
Worldview Dimensions	Mythos: sacred texts, scriptures, narratives, stories	Do you regard any texts, books or stories as sacred, holy, divinely inspired or of central importance? Can you explain why or why not?
	Logos: teachings, doctrines	Do you follow any teachings or beliefs? Can you explain why or why not?
	Ethikos: ethics; ethical principles	How do you decide what is right and wrong? Do you follow any laws or rules?
	Rituals, symbols	Do you participate in any rituals? Do you use any special symbols? Can you explain why or why not?
	Communitas: social; social gatherings of the devotees	Do you participate in any festivals or special social gatherings? Can you explain why or why not? If you do, what are they, how do they make you feel and how do they influence your beliefs and practices?
	Ekstasis: what experiences strengthen the worldview	

which could be asked in RE of Year 5 pupils (aged 9–10) (as represented in the third column of the tables). Together these questions form what we called the 'Worldview Question Framework', which, we believed, provided an accessible and easily applicable conceptualization of a 'worldview' which could enable pupils to recognise, reflect on, understand and articulate their own worldviews.

Pedagogical principles

In stipulating how the Worldview Question Framework should be used in schools, we developed pedagogical principles that were flexible rather than prescriptive. We endorsed a range of possible applications, as the following examples demonstrate. First, in the context of studying specific (non-)religious phenomena, we recognised that particular questions

Table 3.4 WQF 4

Framework 4	Components		Questions
Ontological/ Epistemological	Nature of being	Material: our physical nature Metaphysical: our spiritual nature Origin/future: the beginnings & future of the universe & and humans	What do you think exists and does not exist? What do you think is real and unreal? You can see, hear, touch, smell and/or taste physical things, but do non-physical things exist? Where do you think the world came from? Do you think it had a beginning? Do you think it will have an end? Where did humans come from?
	Nature of our knowing: the certainty of knowledge	Subjective: what role does the subjective play in determining the certainty of truth, truthfulness? Objective: is truth determined objectively? Source: what are the sources of truth and knowledge?	What is true and false? What is fact and fiction? How do you know? What source(s) do you use to decide? What is knowledge? What is belief? What is opinion? What is faith?

Table 3.5 WQF 5

Framework 5	Components	Questions
Primary/Secondary Beliefs, Values and Principles	Pursuit of justice: what is deemed to be just?	What do you think is fair and unfair? How do you decide?
	Dignity of all people: how is it expressed in everyday life?	Do you think everybody is of equal importance?
	Sacredness of life: is all of life sacred? Is human life accorded greater sacredness or value than other forms of life?	Do you think all life is important? Are humans more or less important than other forms of life?
	Equality/diversity: is everyone given equal status; is there a difference in equality between genders?	How far do you think people are the same and different? Do you think all people should be treated equally?
	Openness/tolerance: what is tolerated; what is not tolerated? Is it open to other ways of thinking or believing?	Which beliefs and practices will you put up with? Which beliefs and practices will you NOT put up with?
	Environmental concern	Are you concerned about the environment? Do you do anything to protect it?

could be selected and then innovative teaching and learning activities could be designed to scaffold pupils' thinking about such matters. This would be particularly necessary when the question involves difficult language or requires complex abstract thinking. Second, we acknowledged that it would be possible to teach about (non-)religious phenomena without making an explicit link to the Worldview Question Framework, but then to allow pupils to choose which question they wished to answer in the light of the subject matter they had just encountered. This would avoid a situation in which the teacher always pre-determines the parameters of their pupils' responses to RE curriculum content and thereby potentially inhibits them from responding personally and authentically. Third, we accepted that, rather than teaching about any (non-)religious phenomena, it would be possible, for a given period of time (e.g. some or all of an RE lesson or unit of work), to focus solely on enabling pupils to reflect upon their beliefs, values, meanings, identities and experiences and to construct answers to questions in the Worldview Question Framework. Having done so, teachers could then develop pupils' reflections on, and responses to, their own learning about religion(s) and worldview(s) in the light of their own worldviews rather than the other way around. For pupils to become autonomous self-regulating learners, capable of planning, monitoring and evaluating their own learning about religion(s) and worldview(s), they need to be given time and space to reflect upon and communicate their own worldviews both in isolation from, and conjunction with, RE subject content. Last, we accepted that the questions from the Worldview Question Framework could be asked and answered explicitly or implicitly. For this reason, we advocated the utilisation of a range of teaching and learning activities, a diversity of stimuli (e.g. questions, questionnaires, visual art, role plays, sentenced starters and poetry) and a multiplicity of modes of pupil expression (e.g. writing, pictures and other media).

Can you imagine how you might use these questions in your RE classroom? What things will you consider before introducing them?

Worldview Profiles

Our main pedagogical principle was that each pupil, in some or all RE lessons, and certainly throughout each unit of work, should be expected to produce a Worldview Profile. This was conceived as a form of a reflective diary. The purpose was not to promote a particular religious or secular worldview or to monitor the directionality of pupils' personal, moral and spiritual development. Rather, they were intended to provide a repository in which each pupil would be expected, however explicitly or implicitly, to formulate and record answers to all of the questions posed in the Worldview Question Framework that appears earlier in the text. Thereby, worldview profiling would represent a practical method by which pupils could gain awareness of (or construct) their own worldviews, however rudimentary and incoherent they may be. Moreover, having brought their developing worldviews to consciousness, pupils could then use this designated space to practise articulating their worldviews, to compare and contrast them with those of others and to begin to understand how they influence, or are influenced by, their learning about religion(s) and worldview(s).

We advised that pupils should be given the opportunity, where appropriate, to return repeatedly to the same questions from the Worldview Question Framework and, as they do so, to reflect upon how and why their answers may have changed or stayed the same, bearing in mind that either outcome was acceptable. Also, we advised that if pupils were unwilling or unable to formulate answers, they should be expected to explain why and under what circumstances they would be willing and able to do so.

Importantly, considering the potentially sensitive nature of their contents, we also permitted teachers to decide who would have access to the pupils' Worldview Profiles and the extent to which they, as teachers, would seek to mark or comment (if at all) on the documents. Here we would permit options ranging from Worldview Profiles that were public documents, accessible in the same way as any other school exercise book, and marked by the teacher, on the one hand, to Worldview Profiles that were private documents, anonymized and confidential to the pupils, with no opportunity for teachers to provide feedback, on the other hand.

We were mindful at all times that the kinds of question pupils were being asked to answer were often of a personal nature, and there are a number of important issues to consider in this regard: Are pupils 'safe enough' in the classroom environment to potentially expose themselves in this way?; Is it fair to ask them to engage in this type and level of reflection in school?; Could it be interpreted as interference in what might otherwise be considered private aspects of child development and nurture?; and Are teachers prepared for the possibility of pupils revealing vulnerabilities or sensitive information about the home environment (e.g. alcoholism, abuse or neglect) and would they know how to respond?

Would you be happy to allow your pupils to keep a Worldview Profile private?

Rather than attempt to develop detailed and prescriptive answers to these and related questions, our approach was to highlight the seriousness of such considerations and then trust the professional judgement of the teachers with whom we were working, based on their knowledge of themselves, their pupils and the contexts in which they were working. We relied on them to create RE classroom environments that were safe spaces in which pupils could reflect upon, and respond to, either publicly or privately, subject matter that was potentially personal, sensitive and controversial. Within existing legal and policy frameworks, the parameters otherwise determining the nature and extent of personal reflection that can be demanded of pupils, we argued, are largely child-specific and context-dependent, and therefore best regulated by the professionals in those schools.

Curriculum trial

The participating teachers on the RE-flect project were asked to create a worldview zone and to trial worldview profiling using the Worldview Question Framework. The purpose was to encourage pupils: (1) to recognise, reflect upon, understand and articulate their own worldviews, (2) to compare and contrast their worldviews with those of others and (3) to explain how their worldviews influence, or are influenced by, their learning about religion(s) and worldview(s).

In practice, the Worldview Profiles took the following different formats: paper booklets; plastic folders containing sheets of paper; Microsoft Word files, stored on personal computers, subsequently printed as booklets; and dedicated exercise books. All teachers decided that Worldview Profiles should not be anonymous but should be confidential to their pupil authors (or at least not accessed by anyone other than their pupil authors and their teachers). None of the teachers provided numerical marks, letter grades or written comments on the Worldview Profiles.

Worldview Profiles were structured in a variety of ways; all were based, albeit to differing degrees, on the direct use of questions taken from the Worldview Question Framework. These were presented either simultaneously in a long list or as and when appropriate, bearing in mind the content of the lesson. Some schools did use other stimuli to encourage pupils to reflect on their worldviews.

All pupils demonstrated particularly good levels of engagement with the questions from F1: Personal Identity, using writing and pictures to express thoughts about themselves and their families, friends and schools; and many pupils offered good responses to questions from F2: Ultimate or Existential Questions. F4: Ontological/Epistemological generally posed the greatest difficulty for pupils. Of the few schools that addressed this Framework, most favoured the question regarding the beginning of the world – explained by the majority of pupils as the 'Big Bang' – as opposed to the more complex ontological or epistemological issues. Where these were considered, however, a couple of sophisticated responses occurred. On the subject of what does and does not exist, Debbie wrote,

> I think that love and air are non-physical things but you can't smell or touch or see them but you know when they are there like when someone kisses or hugs someone else they are showing a sign of love towards another person and that air is there because you need air to live.

On the difference between belief and knowledge, Beth wrote,

> When you believe something it may not be really like say I believe that fish can breathe on the top of the water (I don't) it doesn't have to be true. The other reason is that believe [sic] is your own opinion I believe in god but someone else may not. Know is that it is true like I know that $2 \times 1 = 2$ things like that.

Overall, across the frameworks, and in a variety of schools, not all pupils engaged in depth with the questions. The attempts of teachers to encourage pupils to explain their reasoning, by writing such requests into the questions they asked or tasks they set, sometimes failed. George and Matthew, for example, responded to such requests by writing 'No' and 'No, I cannot' respectively. The length of answers written by pupils also varied. Becky, for example, on one occasion gets only as far as 'This week I've been doing … '. Pupils from several schools responded to questions by merely writing 'yes' or 'no' wherever possible. The pupils who produced Worldview Profiles on computer resorted to copying and pasting previous answers. None of these problems were universal. Other pupils managed fuller and more coherent responses, sometimes writing answers that exceeded one page in length, and teachers often reported that pupils previously reluctant to write had engaged with the Worldview Profiles in a surprisingly enthusiastic way. However, literacy levels clearly impacted upon how the Worldview Profiles were completed.

In addition to writing answers to the framework questions, the majority of pupils also drew pictures. One school created opportunities for other alternative responses by providing activity sheets with cloze exercises, sentences to complete and cut and paste phrases relating to pupil beliefs, together with some questions requiring longer answers. A few individual pupils also demonstrated creative engagement with the questions, with Emma attaching a fold-out photograph of her family to one page of her Worldview Profile; and one school asked pupils to represent key aspects of their 'Worldviews' in the form of electronic word clouds.

Unfortunately, our schools were unable to provide opportunities for pupils to re-visit questions which they had previously answered. Therefore, none of the Worldview Profiles evidenced change or continuity over time. Although we recommend that teachers wanting to adopt this approach plan for how to facilitate further reflection on the same questions, perhaps at the beginning and end of the year or after a particular scheme of work.

In several schools, the Worldview Profiles were used primarily as a means of exploring and recording the pupils' own worldviews, with little or no reference to RE curriculum content or learning processes being made explicit within them. This does not mean that such references were not being made either in the pupils' other written work or in classroom discussions. Where an engagement with RE subject content knowledge was evident within Worldview Profiles, it reflected learning about religion(s) rather than knowledge of how their personal worldview influences, and is influenced by, their learning about religion(s).

From the submitted documented evidence, we can conclude that worldview profiling better facilitated pupils' reflection on, and articulation of, their personal worldviews in isolation from the worldviews of others than it did in relation to the worldviews of others. However, our contextual knowledge leads us to conclude that this was a contingent rather than necessary consequence of the approach. Simple practical steps could have been undertaken by the teachers to address this issue, in terms of re-thinking the focus and parameters of the tasks that were set and the extent of the teacher/peer input and formative feedback available.

Conclusion

The curriculum trial of our worldview profiling approach indicates its potential benefits in terms of improving the ability of pupils to recognise, reflect upon, explore and develop their own worldviews. The Worldview Profiles provided pupils with a special confidential space in which they could explore their beliefs, values, meanings, identities and experiences. Many pupils produced some careful and reflective answers, and some openly admitted to having been encouraged to think about questions they had previously not considered. At the same time, the curriculum trial identified practical obstacles that hindered the successful implementation of the underpinning theories and pedagogical principles.

A creative use of questions from the Worldview Question Framework by a few schools led to the inclusion of additional activities which pupils found particularly engaging, but the majority of the teachers were over-reliant on pupils providing written answers to questions taken directly from the Worldview Question Framework. More imaginative teaching and learning activities were required in order to spark pupils' interest in, and scaffold their thinking about, their developing worldviews. Activities involving card sorting, artwork, drama and role play, for example, could have been used as stimuli for class discussion and personal reflection not only within the meta-thinking zone but also within the worldview zone. This may have provided greater inspiration and encouraged deeper engagement.

A number of factors had a bearing upon the development of pupils' abilities to reflect upon and express their own worldviews. Pupils were often expected to articulate responses in writing to some very complex questions, seemingly without any support from their teachers. While some pupils were evidently able to do so, others were not, and we have no way of knowing whether that was due to illiteracy or whether it reflected an inability to recognise, reflect upon and understand their own worldviews. The general expectation of pupils to provide written answers in Worldview Profile books or folders may have shifted the focus of the activity away from 'reflecting' towards 'writing', even though it is not essential in terms of the mental processes associated with recognising, reflecting upon and/or understanding one's worldview. Attention, therefore, needs to be paid to ensuring that all pupils are able to participate fully in the worldview profiling approach, perhaps by investigating and trialling multiple modes of pupil expression as alternatives to written entries in Worldview Profile books. Electronic media (e.g. emails, 'blogs', personal wikis and audio-video diaries), the creative arts (e.g. paintings, collages, music and drama), as well as other presentational modes (e.g. photographs and multiple-choice questionnaires), could help to overcome the literacy problems that some pupils face. Almost any mechanism by which pupils can share Worldview Profiles and enter into dialogue about them is likely to lead to deeper self-reflection and clearer articulation, as well as a greater understanding of, and empathy for, others.

There were also discrepancies in terms of whether or not pupils had been given an opportunity to participate in relevant whole class discussion prior to making an entry into their Worldview Profiles. While this was not stipulated in our pedagogical principles, where evidence of prior group discussion was found in the Worldview Profiles (e.g. 'I think this is wrong because, as our discussion proved … '), the pupils' answers were more thoughtful and detailed than those of pupils where such evidence was lacking. Therefore, although the worldview profiling approach is primarily concerned to promote pupils' reflection upon their own beliefs, values, meanings, identities and experiences, their ability to do so seems to have been greatly enriched when they were given the opportunity to share their worldviews and/or Worldview Profile content with other people for the purposes of eliciting edifying comments and questions. Such discussions can ensure pupils have the conceptual understanding and the vocabulary necessary to enable them to write up their personal reflections with confidence.

Another important factor was the decision of all of the teachers on our project to refrain from providing any numerical marks, letter grades or written feedback on the Worldview

Profiles. This had been mooted as a possibility by the RE-flect project team, on the basis that the documents could be deemed confidential to the pupils, but it was not a recommendation. While pupils clearly appreciated the creation of a private space in which their personal views could be expressed without fear of judgement or ridicule, there are many reasons why formative assessment and feedback would have been beneficial. It would have ensured that pupils had properly understood the set questions and tasks. It would have enabled teachers to address incorrect statements made by pupils about other people's worldviews and religions. Through providing appropriately provocative comments or inserting challenging questions, the teachers would have been able to encourage the pupils to explain, justify, clarify and elaborate upon their points of view. At the most fundamental level, such feedback could consist simply of repeatedly posing the questions 'Why?' or 'Why not?'; for example, why does 'Emily' not believe in the existence of a God or higher being; why does 'Jessica' think community service is an appropriate form of punishment for some offenders; and why does 'Lauren' believe life has no meaning? In this way, pupils would have been discouraged from answering profound questions with a meagre 'yes' or 'no' and encouraged to engage in greater levels of reflection. At the same time, such questioning minimises inappropriate interference by teachers in the formation of pupils' worldviews and allows for any direction of development of thinking or expression. The cultivation of the ability to describe and justify their worldviews, or to explain why they are unwilling or unable to do so, is arguably a fundamental aspect of what it means to be a critically-engaged and religiously literate pupil.

A particular area of difficulty for many pupils was the consideration of ontological and epistemological questions, such as 'What do you think exists?', 'What do you think is real?', 'What is knowledge?', 'What is belief?' and 'What is opinion?' A grappling with such ideas, and in particular with the question of what it means to hold a belief or worldview, is of key foundational importance if pupils are to acknowledge their own beliefs and understand RE as a dialogue between those of differing beliefs. Questions of this nature need to be addressed in greater detail, and for a longer amount of time, than was evidenced in the Worldview Profiles. Indeed, perhaps for no other reason than the sequencing of the frameworks, more time appeared to have been spent on discussing the relatively simple questions in the framework – 1 (Personal Identity) (e.g. 'How would you describe your school?') – than the profound questions in the framework – 4 (Ontological/Epistemological) (e.g. 'What do you think is real and unreal?'). One practical solution would have been to weight the different areas of the Worldview Question Framework unevenly so as to encourage teachers/pupils to spend proportionately more time on the more complex, abstract issues. Another would have been to develop a method by which teachers or pupils could randomly select frameworks or questions. Whatever the approach, pupils need to be given resources to enable them to feel confident addressing such weighty matters. They could, for example, have been provided with activities to introduce them to the relevant vocabulary prior to them being expected to reflect upon these issues within the context of their Worldview Profiles. The teaching of philosophy, or the methods of philosophical inquiry in primary schools, has burgeoned over the past few years, and there are many existing resources which teachers can draw upon to complement and extend this element of worldview profiling.

A question remains regarding the extent to which pupils, even when confidently expressing their own worldviews, are actually conscious of the fact that this is what they are doing. This issue of self-awareness needs to be brought to the fore in order for pupils to both develop metacognition and engage in successful dialogue with those who hold differing beliefs and worldviews. During the project, the Worldview Profiles were not used to compare and contrast pupils' worldviews with those of others. However, we recommend that pupils are given this opportunity through class or small group discussion. In our schools, the relationship between worldview profiling and RE curriculum content and learning processes focused more on pupils' learning about religion(s), but with no clear relationship being established between this learning and the pupils' worldviews. This was almost entirely due to deficiencies in the implementation of our theories and pedagogical principles rather than proof of their inadequacy. Interestingly, in this regard, none of the teachers addressed the framework 5 questions: 'Which beliefs and practices will you put up with? Which beliefs and practices will you NOT put up with?', which would have encouraged pupils to relate their own worldviews to those of others. Overall, additional thought needs to be given to the relationship between worldview profiling and the study of religion(s) and worldview(s), particularly in terms of how the former influences pupils' conceptualisation of, and engagement with, RE curriculum content, their estimation of the personal relevance of the subject matter, their perceptions of their ability to learn and their motivation to do so.

Finally, further consideration is required with regard to the strengths and weaknesses of limiting worldview profiling to particular school years, curriculum Key Stages or educational phases (e.g. primary schooling), and similarly with regard to the benefits and drawbacks of undertaking worldview profiling solely in relation to RE rather than other curriculum subjects. Arguably, worldview profiling needs to occur over the course of pupils' entire school careers, thus enabling them to consider how and why their views have changed and developed over time. The cross-curricular completion of Worldview Profiles, as part of subjects such as English, Geography and Science, may also inspire the development of some stimulating and creative activities, as well as helping to reduce the burden on an already overcrowded primary school curriculum.

Further reading

Commission on Religious Education. (2018) *Final Report: Religion and Worldviews: The Way Forward*. London: Religious Education Council of England & Wales.

Erricker, C., Sullivan, D., Erricker, J., Logan, J. and Ota, C. (1994) 'The development of children's world views'. *Journal of Beliefs and Values*, 15 (2), 3–6.

Pett, S. (Autumn 2018) 'Where do you stand? Insider and outsider views on religion in RE'. *REToday*. 49–55.

Valk, J. (2009a) 'Knowing self and others: Worldview study at Renaissance College'. *Journal of Adult Theological Education*, 6 (1), 69–80.

Wright, A. (2000) 'The Spiritual Education Project: Cultivating spiritual and religious literacy through a critical pedagogy of Religious Education'. In M. Grimmit (ed.), *Pedagogies of Religious Education: Case Studies in the Research and Development of Good Pedagogic Practice in RE*. Essex, UK: McCrimmon Publishing Co. Ltd., 170–187.

Teacher voice 2
Promoting children's views of the world (Jeanette)

As part of the RE-flect project, the participants were asked to include a Worldview Profile for each child. The profile consisted of the following frameworks; Personal Identity, Values and Principals, Big Questions, Worldview Dimensions and Reality and Knowledge. I found the Worldview Profile aspect of the project particularly fascinating, especially regarding the personal development of both the children and myself.

To assist the children, I set up a worldview zone in the classroom. This zone contained poster prompts of the frameworks for the children to focus on, together with word clouds with the words 'Remembering', 'Guessing', 'Believing' and 'Knowing' from the meta-thinking zone, along with several 'thinking' and 'question' pictures, which were pinned around the zone to draw their attention and remind them to reflect.

I decided to introduce the Worldview Profile at the beginning of the RE lesson and explained it would mostly take the form of a personal diary. I emphasised that it was only their own thoughts, beliefs and knowledge which should be recorded and not those of their friends or neighbours. I also suggested that their recordings could be writing, including poems or pictures.

At the beginning of the assignment, the children were quite confident describing themselves, their home life, friends, school, their likes and dislikes. They also were equally happy describing what they thought was right and wrong, good and bad behaviour. At the end of each session, the children used traffic light cards to show how they felt about the task; red for difficult, amber for needed some thought, green for confident.

As the project progressed and the questions became more thought-provoking, the pupils found the tasks more challenging, e.g. when asked – 'Do you think there is a God or a higher being or force or power?' The majority of the pupils wrote that they didn't believe there was. Similarly, with the questions regarding where the world and humans came from. A high percentage of children went into a lengthy explanation of the Big Bang theory and evolution. However, when asked – 'Do you think there is life after death?' – there were only a few children that believed that when people died there was nothing afterwards. The majority of the pupils drew or wrote a description of what Christians would call heaven or something similar.

Although, as previously stated, the answers to the Worldview Profile took the form of a personal diary, on a couple of sessions when the pupils were familiar with the framework, I displayed the question on the whiteboard and the whole class had an open forum discussion. I found this allowed pupils, who struggled with committing their thoughts and beliefs to paper, to participate in the discussions orally so as not feel left out.

By providing the pupils with time and encouragement, they were able to explore their thoughts and beliefs in depth. I felt that this enhanced their interaction and understanding of different faiths in the following RE lessons. In addition, they also began to have a greater understanding of who they were as people in the world.

Resources zone and lesson planning

4

As we stated in the Introduction, the RE-flect project was an attempt to address some of the wider and highly contested issues of RE in primary schools in England. In this chapter we revisit some of these issues, drawing on recent and contemporary debates, including the report produced by the Commission on Religious Education (2018) mentioned in the Introduction. We show how the approach to teaching and learning adopted by the RE-flect project set out to address them, demonstrating how it is coherent with current non-statutory guidance and recommendations. We begin this chapter by focusing on the third zone of the RE-flect project, the resources zone, showing how this was used in different project classrooms to engage pupils in debates about different faiths, drawing on their own experiences and backgrounds. The chapter then provides teachers with a framework for planning lessons using RE-flect principles drawing together the three different zones and the principles outlined in Chapter 1. This framework enables teachers to create their own RE-flect activities to meet the needs of their local context and syllabus. A planning checklist is provided to ensure that sufficient opportunities are provided for the development of pupils' metacognition within the context of each RE lesson. Finally, we consider the issues of initial teacher training and continued professional development.

Resources zone

One way in which the resources zone can be imagined is in reference to a 'nature table'. The zone is a place within the classroom where pupils and teachers can bring together items that they consider to have relevance to the topic being studied. The Commission on Religious Education (2018) includes in its recommendation for a National Entitlement that pupils be taught 'the role of religious and non-religious ritual and practices, foundational texts, and of the arts, in both the formation and communication of experience, beliefs, values, identities and commitments' (2018, p. 12). The resources zone is a place where this teaching can be supported; theological, philosophical and religious ideas can become tangible through the use of appropriate artefacts such as photographs, representations of buildings, texts and other material items related to and representing such ideas.

Pupils might bring in items from home that are relevant to the topic; the zone might also include examples of pupils' work from the lessons; wider resources, such as textbooks (both singly and in collections), posters and/or things that prompt questions, including computer resources such as lists of websites, CDs and DVDs and art materials which can be used in the lessons. In fact, the zone itself could be an entirely 'virtual' construction, through the use of interactive whiteboards, web pages, media clips and so on. It is often possible to arrange for the purchase of religious artefacts to support teaching from a variety of sources, and many local authorities and Diocesan Education Centres offer 'loan boxes' through their support services.

Whilst the size of the resources zone is not itself a major issue, the siting of the zone in a classroom where space is at a premium, combined with the responsibility to take care of the artefacts brought in by pupils, is something to consider carefully. For example, whilst a window ledge might lend itself well to the display of materials that are to be *looked* at, a different position might be more appropriate for artefacts that are designed to be *touched*. Further, if, as suggested in the lesson planning framework that follows, pupils are encouraged to visit the resources zone during lessons, will this be possible without causing disruption to other pupils in the classroom and other activities within the lesson?

In some of the schools we worked with, the resources zone was a permanent fixture. In one or two cases an area was set aside within the classroom itself, so in one of the schools, there was a dedicated table near a reference bookshelf in the corner of the classroom. Here, items could be displayed and accessed easily; pupils were used to moving to and from this area to make use of reference material in other lessons, and there was sufficient circulation space within the classroom for this to happen without any disruption to fellow pupils or the teacher. In another of the schools, where the teacher of RE was not the main classroom teacher, a space was set aside just outside the classroom area in a vestibule area between the corridor and the entry point to two classrooms. The nature of the zone here was necessarily different. As pupils from the wider school passed by frequently, it was a little more difficult to establish the same range of materials because of the potential for interference. However, by establishing the zone here, pupils from the RE classroom were able to make use of the resources when appropriate, and the zone acted as a point of interest for others within the school. Elsewhere, the zone was sometimes less permanent, being set up just for the RE lessons. Deploying this approach led to a little extra work on the teacher's part, but because the objects were only accessible during the RE lesson, it became possible to maintain closer supervision of the objects. As a result, items that may have been felt too precious to leave on permanent display could be included.

We stress that there is no right or wrong way; each classroom environment is different, and the manner in which the resources zone is set up needs to reflect the different practices and spaces available. Further, it may be possible and practicable to have a combination approach;

for example, a display that can be safely left available all the time, with additional objects which require more care and protection being added just for the RE lesson itself. We know that in some school settings, a teacher other than the main class teacher carries responsibility for delivering RE lessons, and we recognise that this raises the need for negotiation over how space is used and who is responsible for it.

For the resources within the zone to have the greatest impact, they need to be relevant to the topic under study. Although the materials gathered in the resource zone can be from a variety of sources, thought should be given to when the materials need to be changed and/or refreshed, especially where topics are changing quite quickly. Sometimes, especially where materials are brought from home, the connections between the items and the topics can be a little unclear. It is incumbent on the teacher to explore these connections, especially where they are not obvious. Pupils could be asked to explain how the object is connected with the topic, or the pupil's perception of the topic; this can also be a fruitful approach where the links appear to be obvious; sometimes things are not as they seem. It can be worthwhile finding out who was involved in the selection of the artefact, as well as the reasons behind its selection. This might be a good moment to involve parents and guardians.

> Where could you put your resource zone? Is there anyone you need to negotiate with to secure a space for it?

The benefits of the resources zone are wider than simply offering a series of artefacts or objects which relate to the topic being studied. Through thoughtful use of the zone, pupils can be encouraged to develop respect (both for the physical objects and the sentiments, feelings and practices they represent and/or portray); the development of multiple perspectives can be enhanced; relationships can be strengthened (through the better understanding of the other and identification of common ground and shared or overlapping experiences); and consequently, a sense of ownership, togetherness and community can be built, each of which is a key component in building a metacognitive environment.

However, great care needs to be taken with those artefacts that have a specifically religious link. Some objects, such as a 'Seder plate', have an educative purpose in their 'religious setting', but there the plate would not be seen as an *artefact*. There is a delicate balance to be achieved between treating artefacts with sensitivity and being oversensitive. Similarly, treating religious artefacts with respect can entail considerations beyond 'looking after' the item; the way in which a teacher or pupil handles a particular object should be considered carefully; balancing the educative purpose of handling the artefact with respect for their religious significance is important (Homan, 2000). To help, Karen Walshe suggests five key questions to consider in using religious artefacts in the classroom, which may be useful in thinking about their role in the resource zone.

> What is my purpose?
> How will using this artefact extend my students' understanding of a particular religious tradition?
> What is the religious/cultural context within which this item is usually used?

How will I portray that to my students?

How will I ensure that my use, and my students' [use] of this artefact, respects the religious significance of this item for members of that faith tradition?

(Walshe, 2011)

By focusing on respect for others and their things, wider lessons about the roles of pupils and appropriate boundaries around the belongings of others can also be drawn out. In addition, questions and tasks relating to how the materials included can help with the task at hand and the processes of learning can give an opportunity for pupils to demonstrate their metacognition.

Furthermore, the selection and subsequent use of the materials gathered provide ample opportunity for reflection. For example, the 'objects' gathered in the resources zone can be used to support pupils in reflecting on the issue of *representation*; noting the differences between, on the one hand, religious and non-religious phenomena and, on the other, tangible representations of them. Thus, there are opportunities to explore issues of selection and sequencing; Why this artefact and not another? How might our understanding be different if we looked at these few items in a different order? How do these items relate to each other? This can aid the questioning of a tendency to present religions and worldviews to pupils as something 'neat and tidy'. The resources zone could be thought of as a sort of 'crowdsourcing' of curriculum content knowledge.

If the classroom community brings together a series of objects that appear contradictory, there is an opportunity to present something of the complexity associated with representation; this in itself can be a metacognitive activity; pupils can be asked probing questions about how they know things and whether other strategies might have been more appropriate. Further, such engagement with resources may allow some questions to be answered whilst further questions arise which are unanswered and which require further research to be undertaken, something which is essential in a metacognitive learning environment. Overall, such an approach liberates pupils from any pretence that knowledge about religions/worldviews and (non-)religious phenomena is unproblematic and incontestable.

The resources zone makes a tangible reality of the question 'what are the objects of study in RE?' In other words, what is *really* being studied? For example, religious experience (broadly understood), in the main, is not about objects *per se* but about concepts, practices, behaviours and beliefs that are expressed, passed on and lived out, with objects often being used to *support* those processes, or to *signify* things about them. These relationships, between the physical objects and questions and topics under scrutiny, can all be drawn out and discussed, and in doing so, reflection on the processes of learning can be included alongside reflection on the content of learning.

Current challenges to RE

As we have already stated, RE in primary schools faces a number of challenges, including those highlighted in a series of Ofsted (Office for Standards in Education, 2007; 2010; 2013) subject reports and the recent final report of the Commission on Religious Education (2018), which identified a number of key areas of concern. Low standards, it is argued, arise from confusion over the purpose of RE, including teachers' lack of subject knowledge and the lack of training available to them. One of the central aspects of the recommended National Entitlement to the Study of Religion and Worldviews, set out by the Commission on Religious Education, is that

> Pupils are ... entitled to be taught by teachers who: 1) have secure subject knowledge; 2) are capable of addressing misconceptions and misunderstandings and handling controversial issues; 3) demonstrate a critical understanding of developments in the study of religion and worldviews and 4) promote the value of scholarship.
>
> (2018, p. 13)

Lack of provision of RE, although an issue more often associated with secondary schools, is associated with the expansion of Academies, and as such it has the potential to affect more primary schools in due course. The Commission on Religious Education (2018) specifically argues that 'the subject must be given adequate time and resources commensurate with the place of Religion and Worldviews as a core component of the curriculum' (2018, p. 13).

The RE-flect project sought to address such current issues, providing teachers with guidance on methods and content and working collaboratively with teachers, including through the provision of continuing professional development, ultimately supporting the development of good RE through the development of a metacognitive environment.

Understanding and articulating what RE is *for* has been, historically, and remains, notoriously difficult (e.g. Teece, 2011). A number of writers have highlighted some persistent myths about the nature of RE, including the existence of a false dichotomy between skills and content (e.g. Blaylock, Gent, Stern and Walshe, 2013), with some suggesting that there needs to be a greater attention paid to the pedagogy of RE than has been the case (e.g. Baumfield, 2010), and the assumption that some concepts or belief systems are too complex or culturally distanced for children at certain ages and stages (e.g. Chater and Erricker, 2013); and the belief that 'Learning about religions' must always precede 'Learning from religion' (Qualifications & Curriculum Authority [QCA], 2004). Further, there has been an ongoing and significant discussion about whether these two Attainment Targets are themselves appropriate (e.g. Blaylock, 2000). In a non-statutory report published in 2013, there is a move away from discussion of RE in terms of the attainment targets of learning about religions and learning from religion. Rather, there is a call for RE to be centred around three aims, which are to (1) know about and understand a range of religions and worldviews; (2) express ideas and insights about the nature, significance and impact of religions and worldviews; and (3) gain and deploy the skills needed to engage seriously with religions and worldviews (Religious Education Council of England and Wales, 2013). However, the vast majority of Agreed Syllabuses (which have a statutory basis) are still based on the two attainment targets, even if sometimes a slightly different nomenclature is used.

According to *Religious Education in English Schools: Non-statutory Guidance 2010* (Department for Children, Schools and Families, 2010, p. 8), RE should:

Provoke challenging questions about the meaning and purpose of life and what it means to be human;
Encourage pupils to explore their own beliefs;
Enable pupils to build a sense of identity and belonging, teaching respect for others;
Encourage pupils to consider their responsibility to self and others;
Contribute to community cohesion by promoting tolerance and encouraging empathy, generosity and compassion; and
Enable pupils to learn about religion and religious faiths as well as learning from them.

Arguably, it is the last of the items on this list which is most clearly specific to RE. Indeed, the other elements could be accomplished through other curriculum subjects. Ofsted found that schools are increasingly losing touch with the idea that RE should be primarily about the study of religion and belief, with some schools avoiding 'in-depth studies of religions and belief'.

Lesson planning framework

The RE-flect approach restores a focus on (non-)religious beliefs, practices and values, providing pupils with opportunities to engage with these and encouraging 'pupils to explore their own beliefs' (Department for Children, Schools and Families, 2010, p. 8) through facilitating and supporting their reflection on their own beliefs and values. In short, good learning about religion(s) and worldview(s) necessitates careful thinking on the part of the learner about the impact of their positionality on what they learn and how they learn; pupils explore their own beliefs to become better at learning about religions and worldviews and vice versa.

This development of pupils' ability to reflect on their own beliefs and values before, during and after encountering those of other worldviews, in a cyclical and parallel way, has been particularly identified in Ofsted documents as a crucial element in RE (Office for Standards in Education, 2013, p. 14), as well as in the more recent Commission on Religious Education (2018). The worldview zone, discussed in Chapter 3, focuses on these issues. In their Worldview Profiles, pupils became better at writing descriptive material about themselves and then at writing critical reflections on philosophical issues and vice versa. We consider that there is a link between pupils' worldviews and their learning (their study) rather than between their worldviews and the material they are studying. To some extent, they are one and the same, but it is the impact upon learning that we have focused on within this project.

A metacognitive classroom environment can facilitate such reflection through the provision of opportunities for pupils to explain their own thinking and discuss their learning and the learning process. Enabling pupils to develop an appropriate vocabulary and language of thinking is vital to this, something which can be supported by the explicit use, by the whole classroom community, of metaphors and images for learning. The RE-flect project shows that the development of the metacognitive environment is linked to positive outcomes in terms of academic skills, attainment and self-regulated learning. We also found some positive movement in terms of tolerance, listening and discussing and (in one case) better behaviour.

Beyond the creation of the metacognitive environment, there are some types of activity, as discussed in Chapter 1, that particularly support the creation of metacognitive experiences. These include complex tasks which require planning, collaboration and decision-making. However, to make the lesson flow as well as possible, these ideas need incorporation at an early stage in the planning process rather than being added in afterwards. Other issues which need to be thought about early in the process are how to build on prior learning, how to facilitate social interaction and how best to support pupils in developing an awareness of their own learning.

Alongside their criticisms and concerns discussed earlier, Ofsted offers suggestions for improvement. The 2010 report calls for more genuine investigation in RE. It notes that where RE is most effective, it uses a range of 'enquiry skills' such as investigation, interpretation, analysis, evaluation and reflection, but suggests that this use is not embedded sufficiently into classroom practice (Office for Standards in Education, 2010). The RE-flect approach coheres with these suggestions, with an emphasis on enabling pupils to reflect on how they are learning, the challenges they face and the ways in which they might improve their learning in RE.

> Could you provide more opportunities for pupils to reflect on their own beliefs and values? Could you provide more opportunities for pupils to reflect on their learning?

The 2013 Ofsted report makes similar suggestions, emphasising the importance of inquiry-based learning. It specifically recommends that such an approach, (1) 'starts by engaging pupils in their learning' (Office for Standards in Education, 2013, p. 23), not just at an early stage, or at the beginning of a topic or lesson, but throughout the learning process; (2) allows time for reflection; (3) 'enables pupils to reconsider their initial thinking and extends their enquiry as they begin to see new levels of possibility' (ibid, p. 24). This concentration on pupils being engaged in, and taking responsibility for, their own learning, together with an emphasis on sustained learning, is at the heart of the RE-flect approach.

This Ofsted subject report for RE (Office for Standards in Education, 2013) demonstrates that an approach to RE which is inquiry-based is not opposed to the transmission of knowledge. Rather than a focus on processes of learning working against the transmission of knowledge, the combination enables pupils to think more carefully about the representation of religions and worldviews and the resources used to represent them. The selection and sequencing of knowledge content, and the resources used to teach that content, are active decisions that have generally been made by the teacher. We are subverting that somewhat by expecting pupils to contribute, to select resources, to think about why they have done so, to think about what they tell us and what they do not. Thus, they grow in understanding that the knowledge thereby acquired is only ever partial.

In summary, the development of the type of metacognitive classroom environment that the RE-flect approach encourages can support good RE by providing opportunities to:

- Enable pupils to build on prior learning in a sustained manner;
- Support pupils in taking responsibility for their learning and their thinking;
- Facilitate social interaction motivated by learning;
- Encourage an active exchange of ideas between teachers and pupils;
- Promote thoughtful and reflective dialogue;
- Enable pupils to develop a language of thinking;
- Make explicit use of metaphors and images for learning;
- Promote discussion about learning and the learning process;
- Provide opportunities for pupils to explain their own thinking;
- Provide opportunities for pupils to reflect on their own beliefs and values;
- Provide an opportunity for pupils to engage with (non-)religious beliefs, practices and values;
- Enable pupils to reflect on how they learn in RE and the challenges they face; and
- Enable pupils to reflect on how they might improve their learning in RE.

Like any other lesson, a metacognitive lesson needs to have a clear aim or focus. We have found that asking a question is often a good way to begin; this is not necessarily an Intended Learning Outcome to be shared with the class at the outset of the lesson but is a clear and explicit question that will guide both the lesson planning and the lesson delivery. In many cases, this might be taken from the syllabus or another appropriate scheme of work.

So, you might begin with a reflection on their own knowledge in relation to the question. What do you know about the topic? How do you know this? What do you need to find out?

These questions are also valid entry points for discussion with the pupils you are working with. In fact, having asked them of yourself, you will be able to share your learning insights with your pupils, thus modelling your own thinking processes. Asking pupils directly about the aim of the task, the goal and how the task can be tackled is also important; you might ask the class how they could find answers to their questions; How are we going to tackle this task?

Another set of questions centres on how the answer to the key topic question differs according to the position of the questioner. Going beyond the question, e.g. 'Does this topic question matter to you?' You might then explore whether the question could be viewed differently depending on the worldview held. This would facilitate the development of a theory of mind, i.e. an ability to understand how others think and view the world. Example questions could include: Might the question be more/less important if you had friends or relatives who held a particular worldview? Might the question have a different relevance if you had a religious/non-religious worldview? Asking these sorts of questions also encourages pupils to reflect on how their own worldviews and 'starting point' impact on the way in which they view the worldviews and starting points of others. Later in the lesson, or sequence of lessons, these kinds of questions can be asked again, giving opportunities for pupils to reflect on how their own worldviews may have changed or developed, thus providing opportunities for pupils to reflect on their worldviews and to visit and engage with the materials/resources in the three zones. This can also include 'time out' spaces within the lesson where pupils are encouraged to quietly reflect on their thinking and their learning. It can be helpful to use prompt questions to facilitate this. For example, you might include some of the questions from the meta-thinking zone (see Chapter 2) and draw inspiration from the material in Chapter 5.

Taking this sort of direction gives the pupils some involvement in the direction that the lesson takes and the way in which it develops. There might be an opportunity here to include the resource zone, both in terms of referring to material that is present there and also in terms of what might be added to the zone to enrich the resources available.

As you think about appropriate activities for the lesson, what activities can you include that will give pupils the opportunity to take greater responsibility for their own learning? Perhaps in approaching the questions already listed, you might explore the issue of strategies to answer them, considering why some strategies might be better than others.

In line with the explanation of metacognition set out in Chapter 1, we suggest a focus on activities that are complex, open-ended and that require decisions to be made. These sorts of conditions promote reflection on how tasks are approached, how responses are justified and how decisions are made.

One good example of this is a roleplay lesson in which pupils are invited to imagine they are participating in a public consultation. The scenario is that six different interest groups (e.g. Muslim, Hindu, Catholic, Humanist, Hospital Chaplain and Interior Decorator) are asked to design a new hospital chapel. These designs are to be presented to the Hospital's Building Manager (the teacher in the role). Initially, pupils are divided into the six different groups and given information about their new identities and their priorities, e.g. Interior Decorators want a modern design using fashionable styles; the faith groups wish the space to reflect their particular beliefs and practices. Each group uses images of example chapels, places of worship and/or religious buildings, as well as other sources of information to generate a 'wish list' for the new build. At this point in the learning sequence, the existing groups are disbanded and new groups are created. Each group now comprises a representative from each of the six interest groups. Each of the new groups must design a chapel with which all members are happy. At the end of the session, each group must present their ideas to the Hospital's building manager (teacher in the role) who will give feedback on each design and choose the winning proposal. The groups are told that the building manager is looking for creative compromises, inclusive ideas and a low-cost modern design/style.

During and/or after such complex, open-ended and problem-based activities, pupils can be asked questions about their learning: What did you learn from engaging in that task? What questions do you still have about the topic? Do you think you understood the task and what it sought to teach you? How do you know that you have understood? Could you have done the task differently? Has today's lesson made you think differently in any way? By asking questions, both as part of the activity and as part of the plenary sessions, reflection *on learning* becomes an integral part of the process of learning rather than an 'add-on', and pupils are given the opportunity to demonstrate metacognition.

It will become clear to you when pupils are demonstrating metacognition when their self-questioning becomes more explicit, when they use mental state words reflectively, when it is clear and explicit that they are monitoring and controlling their thinking (perhaps by planning in advance and/or evaluating the effectiveness of a strategy or task), when they show awareness of their own beliefs and values and how these relate to those of others.

In many of the activities that have been developed for and during the project (see Chapter 5), there is an emphasis on collaborative work between pupils. This develops a sense of social metacognition (discussed in Chapter 1), which helps us understand the viewpoint of others, a central skill in RE. Group work allows for the development of authentic collaboration, whereby a team works together in the pursuit of a common goal, allowing everyone to feel that they are involved in the activities and providing a safe space where learning, including through making mistakes, can take place. As in any other case, careful thought regarding the make-up of such groups will be important.

> What activities do you currently do that you could reuse? What aspects are missing from your current approach? How could you develop them?

Table 4.1 provides a framework and a checklist for RE-flect lesson planning. This can be transferred to other lesson planning across curriculum subjects and age groups. It is designed to focus your attention on activities which specifically facilitate the development

Table 4.1 Lesson planning framework checklist

Lesson		Date	Time
Element		Met Y/N?	How will this element be met?
Focus question			
Opportunities for collaborative work			
Pupils reflect on existing knowledge, source of this knowledge and evaluation of this knowledge			
Pupils consider how the answer to the focus question might be important to them and to others			
Pupils reflect on how their own worldviews and 'starting point' impact on the way in which they view the worldviews and starting points of others			
Pupils take responsibility for their learning, including reflecting on how to approach the focus question and evaluation of learning strategies			
Pupils reflect on their own worldviews and how this might change during the lesson			
'Time out' spaces where pupils are encouraged to think about their thinking and their learning			
Pupils visit and engage with material/resources in the three zones			
Opportunities for pupils to demonstrate metacognition			
Gather evidence that pupils have employed metacognitive strategies during the lesson			

of metacognition, and as such, the lesson planning complements the metacognitive question cards described in Chapter 2 and the Worldview Question Framework described in Chapter 3. By providing opportunities for each of the elements in the table, you will facilitate metacognitive development of your pupils, and this should lead to increased self-regulated learning as well as a deeper understanding of the purpose of RE.

Teacher training and teacher CPD

Although the 2013 Ofsted report highlights 'weaknesses in teaching', a little unpacking of the report shows that the focus is actually on weaknesses in teachers' understanding of the subject, compounded by limited access to effective training (Office for Standards in Education, 2013, pp. 9–10). An earlier report suggests that pupils' achievement in RE is heavily dependent on individual teachers (Office for Standards in Education, 2007). There, Ofsted suggests that the key factor inhibiting achievement is teachers' (particularly primary school teachers') lack of understanding of the content and pedagogy of the subject.

The Religious Education Council's *A Review of Religious Education in England* (2013) reported that, whilst there was a plethora of guidance to teachers about the aims and purposes of the subject, the guidance often failed to enable teachers to resolve a tension between the academic goal of extending and deepening pupils' ability to make sense of religion and belief and the wider goal of contributing towards their overall personal development (Office for Standards in Education, 2013). However, we would argue that to set this up as a tension is unhelpful. Extending and deepening pupils' ability to make sense of religion and belief through RE contributes to the wider goal of contributing towards their overall personal development.

Potentially compounding this issue is the degree to which many pupils, especially those in primary schools, are taught RE by non-specialists, something that was reflected in the variety of teachers involved in the RE-flect project. The All-Party Parliamentary Group (APPG) on RE report recorded that 'in over half of the 300 schools participating in [their study], some or all pupils were taught RE by someone other than their class teacher. In a quarter of these … RE was taught by teaching assistants' (APPG, 2013, p. 4). Even where RE was taught by those with some RE-related training or qualification, around 50% lacked confidence in teaching the subject and 'about half of subject leaders in primary schools lack the expertise or experience to undertake their role effectively' (APPG, 2013, p. 4).

Initial teacher training courses for the primary phase were also found to provide little training to non-specialist RE teachers (APPG, 2013), and however good later professional development opportunities might be, they could not compensate for this initial lack. Further, there is a danger in such marginalisation of the subject during initial teacher education that an implicit understanding will develop that RE is not something to be taken seriously. The Commission on Religious Education (2018) makes recommendations which have the potential to significantly affect this situation. In order to effectively implement the National Entitlement, the Commission recommends that trainee teachers need sufficient time devoted to Religions and Worldviews in their training year to adequately prepare them. Specifically, they recommend that 'There should be a minimum of 12 hours of contact time for Religion and Worldviews for all forms of primary ITE including School Direct and other school-based routes' (2018, p. 47), with further recommendations regarding bursaries for trainees and funding for Subject Knowledge Enhancement courses.

The current situation is perhaps exacerbated by a lack of opportunity in Continuing Professional Development (CPD). For example, the All-Party Parliamentary Group Report states that 'in nearly 40% of schools RE teachers have inadequate access to continuing professional development' (APPG, 2013, p. 26), leading to the criticism that teachers lacked subject knowledge and failed to explore the changing political and social significance of religion in the modern world. Ofsted also identifies the lack of provision of CPD as a significant issue (Office for Standards in Education, 2010, p. 25). The extent to which this limited accessibility to CPD affects non-specialists and/or teaching assistants is currently under-researched.

However, attempts are being made to address these issues, especially the supply of appropriate CPD opportunities. Many local Dioceses and Local Authorities offer training and support, as does the National Association of Teachers of Religious Education (NATRE). RE Today Services offer training events across the country and publish a wide range of resources and support materials through the *RE Today* magazine and online. In many areas now, local learning 'hubs' of RE teachers have formed, often including Higher Education partners, which also provide CPD opportunities, frequently through termly twilight meetings and annual conferences. Many of these hubs are teacher-led and are very responsive to training needs identified within their make-up. There are also virtual networks, including support from RE:online (www.reonline.org.uk/supporting/) and online communities that meet through social media (for example, an online structured chat on Twitter with the hashtag #rechatuk).

The Commission on Religious Education (2018) makes specific recommendations in regard to CPD, arguing that central government funding should be made available for a period of at least five years to support the development of national and local provision of CPD, including online material (such as static online resources and massive open online courses, also known as MOOCs) and local face-to-face groups and networks, including the expansion and maintenance of hubs (2018, p. 49).

Conclusion

This chapter has described and illustrated the resources zone and raised some questions about how this zone might be incorporated successfully in the classroom. It has shown how the RE-flect approach responds to current issues in the primary RE classroom and how it is coherent with many current guidance documents. A planning framework is set out, with an easy to refer to checklist to support teachers in the planning of metacognitive RE lessons. The next chapter, Chapter 5, discusses the way in which this framework has been taken up in one practitioner's classroom, exemplifying the approach through a variety of activities.

Further reading

All-Party Parliamentary Group for Religious Education. (2013) *RE: The Truth Unmasked: The Supply of and Support for Religious Education Teachers*. London: All-Party Parliamentary Group for Religious Education and The Religious Education Council of England and Wales. Online. http://religiouseducationcouncil.org.uk/appg/news/2013-03-18/appg-re-final-report-the-truth-unmasked.

Department for Children, Schools and Families. (2010) *Religious Education in English Schools: Non-statutory Guidance*. Nottingham, UK: Department for Children, Schools and Families.

Homan, R. (2000) 'Don't let the Murti get dirty: The uses and abuses of religious 'artefacts'. *British Journal of Religious Education*, 23 (1), 27–37.

Office for Standards in Education. (2013) *Religious Education – Realising the Potential*. Manchester, UK: Office for Standards in Education.

A practitioner's approach 5

The author in context

Despite being a Specialist Leader of Education (SLE) for RE, I do not have specialist qualifications in the subject or any of its related disciplines. In this respect, I am in the same position as the majority of primary school teachers. I have developed experience and associated expertise in the delivery of RE in the primary setting from teaching it across at first Key Stage 2 (7–11-year-olds) and now Key Stage 1 (5–7-year-olds).

I first became aware of the RE-flect project when invited in my capacity as an AST (Advanced Skills Teacher) to sit on the steering committee for the project. As the project proceeded, it transpired that the teachers and teaching assistants working with the team would benefit from the provision of some exemplar lessons. The lessons needed to be compatible with the project's theoretical framework and demonstrate how RE could be 'meta-cognitively-orientated'. I needed to do some research!

Designing the right type of activity

The conditions under which metacognition might develop are outlined in Chapter 1, and I had witnessed such conditions created in the context of team-building activities and problem-solving activities. It became my intention to attempt to identify what made these activities successful and a fertile ground for developing metacognition. I identified that most successful sessions opened with 'icebreaker' activities and trust exercises. When this was effectively led, pupils felt safe. Thus, they were willing to communicate their ideas, were open to suggestion and constructive criticism and unafraid to take risks. In such activities, whether it was transporting a bucket of water across a series of obstacles, constructing the tallest tower they could from newspaper or ordering stones according to size, pupils cared about the outcomes. This was sometimes helped or hindered by a competitive dimension as their group competed with others. As the pupils cared about their outcomes, they were more likely to think before they acted. Their desire to win or succeed made the actions of the group weighty and in some cases risky as they endeavoured to go faster, higher, further or generate a better approach than other teams.

The best examples of such activities presented pupils with challenges they had never attempted before. Novelty, challenge and fun was added through:

Specifying goals or renewed goals for the challenge (e.g. making a bridge, tower, vehicle capable of performing in a certain way or under particular circumstances).
Altering the type of resources available (e.g. only using spaghetti and marshmallows!).
Adding constraints and adjusting the rules of the task (e.g. working without talking or blindfolded!).

These types of activities have often had a number of things in common.

1. They have one clear goal, which is easy to understand and assess one's progress towards. For example, one such activity is to make a parachute which will protect an egg from breaking only using the resources available. The concept of a parachute is easy to grasp, as is the idea of stopping an egg from breaking. Success is easy to assess, based on the well-being of the egg after its descent to the floor.
2. They are designed to be collaborative activities where three or more people co-construct a way forward. Such activities can often be completed in a number of different ways and can be attempted by all, regardless of ability.
3. They are governed by rules and constraints. These constraints on groups and individuals can range from a simple time limit to a number of complex rules.
4. They often require the innovative use of an unusual selection or combination of resources/materials to use.
5. They often seem simple at first, but reveal technical, strategic and sometimes philosophical complexity as pupils work through them.

This begged the question: what kinds of RE activity could be designed which share some or all of these characteristics? The first step was to consult each school's long-term rolling programme and/or the locally Agreed Syllabus and affiliated schemes of work. After identifying what was due to be taught in the forthcoming unit, it was then necessary to consider what kind of a goal or outcome the class could work towards over the course of the unit. The goal/outcome selected needed to be something pupils could create in collaboration with one another. What follows is a list of such ideas:

- A model of a place of worship
- A plan for a festival
- A museum of a religion

- A ritual to remember something
- An act of charity
- A calendar
- A greetings card
- A shrine
- A piece of art
- A plan for a pilgrimage
- A course of action in relation to a dilemma
- A judgement
- A project
- A presentation
- A script

Many of these ideas seemed viable. Although, many also presented the possibility of the RE being sidelined in favour of the technical skills required to make the item listed. There is, of course, some potential for cross-curricular work here, but only if the RE element is suitably 'ring-fenced'.

These tasks can be completed for any of the following reasons:

- To assess what pupils know already (Formative Assessment)
- To assess what pupils now know (Summative Assessment)
- To give purpose and relevance to the unit of work
- As a means of eliciting pupils' worldviews

> Is this like anything you currently do in RE? What is your experience of requiring pupils to collaborate to complete projects/outcomes using their knowledge and understanding of religion(s)?

However, challenging pupils to work on collaborative projects requires some thought. Collaborating pupils will not have the same worldview, and in some cases these may be diametrically opposed. This can be a good source of social 'cognitive conflict' (Piaget, 1975), requiring pupils to find a way to complete the task that satisfies all members of the group. This requires good group monitoring and control. An alternative method would be to group children according to their worldview. This may solve the conflict issues but could also be divisive and also suggests that the worldview is stable and fixed. Pupils could be allowed to plan their own ideas separately and only then collaborate and discuss how or whether they can be combined into a final outcome. Yet all of these solutions seem somewhat unsatisfactory; a better solution may be not to use these collaborative activities for the purposes of communicating personal beliefs. One example of how this may be avoided can be seen in the activity: *Believe-it-or-not!*

Activity 1: Believe-it-or-not!

When I joined the project, a few example materials had been previously prepared by the team. This activity required pupils to rank belief statements given to them (or self-generated) according to how certain they were of them, with the truest at the top of the list and the least true at the bottom. This apparently simple task can quickly result in discussions about how we know things, what evidence we can rely on, the role of logic and how much evidence we require before we can state something is true. It can also lead to discussions about the nature of different assertions, e.g. is the statement 'there is a pencil on the table' the same kind of statement as 'there is a God'? Although these discussions are best conducted collaboratively, the initial ranking of items needs to be done individually. In sharing these thoughts with others, pupils engage in meta-cognitive discussions about the nature of knowledge (epistemology) and the nature of reality (ontology).

> How would this fit with the way you teach RE? Does this approach worry you at all?

This first example draws heavily on the worldview zone. However, I wanted to find a solution to the issue of how to develop collaborative tasks which did not put pupils in positions where they felt pressure to compromise in relation to their beliefs and values. One solution to this was the creation of board games. Board games share many of the characteristics of the collaborative activities I identified earlier. Board games often have one clear goal – to win! They have rules which limit what people can do and require creative, strategic decisions. They also often provide a limited number of cards/money/time, etc. to achieve the goal. Furthermore, although the examples I am about to share do not require collaboration, they do require cooperation and communication between competing parties. Finally, and particularly with these RE games, they appear simple, but reveal through playing technical, strategic and sometimes philosophical complexity. Here are two examples of such games: *SACRIFICE: The Ultimate Trading Game* and *The Meaning of Christmas*.

Activity 2: SACRIFICE: The Ultimate Trading Game

The aim of this activity is to enable pupils to understand the meaning of the word 'sacrifice' and the challenges inherent in sacrificing something you value. This level of insight can then be used to recognise the significance of religious sacrifices and the causes for which they are made. This activity is in the form of a card game. Players trade cards with one another as they seek to hold the cards they value the most. Each card has a picture of an item which is known to be commonly seen as valuable. They include items ranging from computer consoles, holidays, the ability to read and the well-being of your family to your own life. The activity helps pupils to identify what is truly important to them and enables them to reflect on their values. Pupils can be invited to think about which items they would never part with and those they were surprised to find themselves less attached to. The lesson paves the way for further work on the notion of sacrifice in the context of religious acts such as Jesus' crucifixion and the acts of the Panj Pyare at the founding of the Khalsa.

The rules

The aim of this three–four player card game is for pupils to finish the game with the most valuable 'hand' of cards they can. Pupils begin with seven cards, which they lie out in front of them for everyone to see. The leftover cards are left in a pile in the centre of the table, face down. One card is turned over so that all players can see it in the discard pile. Pupils take turns to select a card from either the face-down pile or the discard pile. They add it to their existing hand and decide which item they are willing to sacrifice. They must complete this transaction whilst saying, 'I am going to sacrifice … for … (the item they kept) because … '. If they discard the new card, then they say, 'I am not willing to sacrifice any of my items for … because … '. They have now completed the first part of their go. They must then look at the rest of the players' 'hands' in order to find an item better than one of their own. They do this in order to propose a transaction; so identifying something they want, but which the other player does not, is strategically important. To make the proposed transaction, they must say: 'Would you be willing to sacrifice your … for my … '. If the answer is *no*, then nothing happens; if the answer is *yes*, then a transaction takes place. Play then moves to the next person sitting to the right. The second player completes both actions, choosing a card from the centre pile and discarding one, and then asking another player for a swap. Play continues until either all cards in the centre are used or a designated time limit is over. Then pupils take turns to explain why they think they have won or lost, i.e. why their hand of cards now represents what is most valuable to them. In a variation on this activity, each pupil first gives each item a score depending on how valuable they judge it to be. At the end of the game, they can calculate their total score and evaluate their success by comparing this to their initial personalised score sheet.

Activity 3: The Meaning of Christmas

The aim of this three–four player card game is for pupils to finish the game with the most personally significant 'hand' of cards they can. Pupils begin with five cards, which they lie out in front of them for everyone to see. The leftover cards are left in a pile in the centre of the table, face down. One card is turned over so that all players can see it in the discard pile. Each card has a picture of an item which is commonly associated with Christmas. The items have been drawn from Christian, secular and pagan traditions. Pupils take turns to select a card from either the face-down pile or the discard pile. They add it to their existing hand and decide whether they want to swap it for any they already have. Pupils are asked to explain why one item is more important to them at Christmas time than the other. After they have done this, the play passes to the player on their right. After this time-limited activity, the pupils should be given the opportunity to reflect on how well they have done and how well their selection reflects what they value about Christmas. A variation on this game requires pupils to compete, not simply in terms of collecting cards of value to them, but also in terms of the quality of their justification. Prior input into what makes a high-quality justification is worthwhile. When pupils are challenged to say something true, relevant to the topic and supported by reasoning, they are forced to spend more time reflecting on their worldview and knowledge of the topic. Pupils can vote for a winner based on who gave the justifications (giving a justification for their choice of course), as long as they know that they cannot vote for themselves. I have found communicating votes and accompanying justifications can be successfully done via individual mini whiteboards.

At this point, I wish to give two warnings. The first is as follows: The activities I have described so far can be conducted in a more or less metacognitive manner. To do these activities is not the same as facilitating metacognition. They simply provide fertile ground for its development. They are the 'grow-bag', not the 'fruit'. Later in this chapter, I will outline how I have had the greatest success facilitating metacognition in these contexts. For now, though, here is my second warning: Even when these activities have proven to be rich in respect to metacognition, they can be 'RE-content poor'. The theoretical framework of the RE-flect project emphasizes pupils' 'worldviews' for the purposes of improving pupils' capacity to engage with learning about religion(s) and worldview(s), rather than an end in itself. To repeatedly plan 'content-lite' RE lessons on the basis that your aim is to develop the pupils' Worldview Profiles will not achieve this aim. Worldview profiling needs to be in parallel with, and/or in preparation for, learning about religion(s) and worldview(s).

Thus, to meet the expectation of the RE syllabus, I needed to find a way to design activities which met the criteria I had established and furthered pupils' understanding of religions, not simply their own worldview and not simply the development of metacognition. One solution to this was to design scenarios where pupils were required to take on a role: looking from another person's perspective. The following example exemplifies this:

Activity 4: The Meaning of Christmas (Extension task)

After pupils have completed *The Meaning of Christmas Game* (Activity 3), the pupils are told that they are to play again, but this time they will be playing from another person's point of view using a *Character Card*. The character cards reflect a range of views about Christmas, including secular cynical viewpoints, secular sympathetic viewpoints, differing Christian viewpoints and a pagan viewpoint. For example, one player may adopt the role of a Christian who believes that Christmas is a time for celebrating God's love for everyone including the poor and unlucky, whereas another player may adopt the position of a Christian who thinks that Christmas is a time for celebrating the arrival of a promised king. Another player may adopt a Pagan outlook believing that Christmas is a time for celebrating the passing of the shortest day of the winter, the victory of the sun over darkness and the renewal of life; at the same time as someone else takes a secular view of Christmas, holding the view that Christmas is purely a time for coming together as a family.

On the second play, pupils have to collect the cards with items which best reflect the priorities of their designated character. Pupils explain their reasoning whilst picking up and putting down their cards with reference to their 'character descriptor'. At the end of the game, pupils can take turns to explain why they think they did or did not succeed with reference to their character description. Another way of playing is for all pupils to play as the same character, enabling a single viewpoint to be explored. Pupils can use their knowledge of the Christmas story and religious symbolism to take cards that others might not recognise or see the relevance of whilst teaching them about the link that they have made.

In this adaption of *The Meaning of Christmas* game, I shifted the focus from the individual's worldview to developing a better understanding of differing viewpoints, including those of religious people. In this respect, this game suits the purposes of:

- Assessing what pupils know already (Formative Assessment)
- Assessing what pupils now know after a unit of learning (Summative Assessment)

The idea of evaluating something from someone else's perspective (developing theory of mind) became another useful device as I began to explore collaborative activities suitable for RE. Instead of pupils constructing a shrine based on their own values or a place of worship to suit all members of the group, the pupils are asked to create the outcome for a particular audience. This task can perform the assessment roles outlined earlier or be the central focus/purpose of all the learning in the unit of work. This requires pupils to take another perspective and monitor their decision-making in relation to a set of success criteria. It also ensures that pupils are operating at a higher level in relation to learning about religion(s) and worldview(s) as they engage with the beliefs and practices associated with the religion/worldview being studied. It is also apt for use as a means of exploring denominational differences.

In a second example, I can show you how this approach can be used differently. Here, rather than requiring children to understand the implications of religious beliefs, they are being introduced to theological concepts. The basic idea for this collaborative group exercise is that they are going to design a throne for Jesus. However, the twist is that they are simply going to be told that they are required to build a throne for a king who is coming to save them. I did this in order to elicit the pupils' understanding of what a king is and who might save them. Once the pupils have articulated their own understanding of kingship and saviours, the religious interpretation can be seen alongside. This can then make it possible to draw comparisons between the two (or however many have been expressed). A more detailed recount of this lesson in action follows:

Activity 5: Throne together: Preparations for a king

In these two lessons, pupils were asked to construct a throne for a king. We conducted the construction process outside using sticks, twine, tarpaulins and scrap materials. The activity can be equally successful using collage materials for a plan. To increase the sense of novelty, the pupils were told a story of enslaved ants being ruled over by grasshoppers. The pupils were told that they were the ants and through role-play began to co-construct a back story explaining why the situation was so, how long it had gone on for and how they felt about it. The pupils, now ants, were informed by another ant (a pupil in the role) that they have had a vision of an ant called SAVIOUR arriving to save them and become their king. The pupils were told that they really wanted this to be true and are invited to make suggestions as to how to get ready for this king. Once the ideas had been generated, the pupils were invited to design and make a throne for their king.

This story mirrors in a simplistic and generalised way the Jewish beliefs about a Messiah, the role of prophets such as Elijah and common ideas about the Jewish attitudes to the Roman occupation of Israel at the time of Jesus. The re-contextualisation of this situation in a made-up story also created a sense of freedom: the pupils (now ants) are free to be characters, not themselves, and to take risks when suggesting and experimenting with ideas for their throne. Pupils began to plan, monitor and assess their thinking and collaborative group work in relation to the design and construction of a throne in preparation for the arrival of a king and saviour. They were asked to reflect on how their beliefs about what they expect from a king/a saviour/a throne and their collaboration affected their performance and decision-making. In a subsequent session, the 'ants' are told that the 'Ant King: SAVIOUR' who has come to save them refused each and every one of the thrones. Pupils were invited to suggest reasons why. Once answers were aired, pupils were told that SAVIOUR would have only accepted a throne if it was plain and boring, like any other chair, was put in the poorest area of the city, could be given up for anyone to sit on – even criminals and people others did not like – and was accompanied with some water for him to wash the feet of the person put on it.

The 'ants' were invited to explain their feelings and ideas as to why SAVIOUR would behave in such a manner. Following this feedback, the parallel story of Elijah's prophesy and the events of Palm Sunday were shared. Pupils were challenged to spot the parallels from the ant story and to provide a short list of the kinds of things the Gospels tell us Jesus did which justify his Christian title, the 'Servant King'.

> What difficulties can you see with this approach? What benefits can you see to this approach?

This lesson plan draws on techniques originally developed by Dorothy Heathcote in the 1970s as expressed in the pedagogy 'Mantle of the Expert', where pupils are reconceived as a team operating in a fictional context completing a commission for a fictional client in collaboration with the teacher. An introductory text is listed as further reading at the end of the chapter. Metacognition is central to the approach as adopted in RE-flect, as the teacher is able to use the fictional context to pause, step out of and, if necessary, rewind time to invite pupils' scrutiny onto their own actions and the actions of others in relation to the rationale/plausibility/success of the emerging narrative, the pupils' learning and to make plans in relation to each.

Facilitating metacognition through the activities: Asking the right question at the right time

Earlier I forewarned the reader that task design alone would not necessarily facilitate metacognitive thought from the children. It may well provide a fertile ground for such reflection to grow, but it also needs to have the right climate and cultivation. The creation of a worldview zone, resource zone and meta-thinking zone can provide pupils with both a manifestation of each of the areas upon which they are being asked to reflect, a place to go to conduct that element of their learning and a useful prompt as to what types of questions and thoughts belong to each aspect of their learning. Like other teachers on the project, finding space for three separate displays in the context of a primary classroom proved a problem; however, I did find that it was possible to use one display board (subdivided into three) to communicate the essence of the three strands. Referring to these visual reminders throughout the learning helped to prompt pupils' own reflection in terms of considering their next steps and reflecting more deeply on what has been learnt. Further to this, having meta-thinking and Worldview Profile questions continually on display normalised these types of questions and allowed me as a teacher to encourage pupils to choose their own reflection question to answer, thus shifting the onus for reflection onto the children.

However, I knew from working with individuals and groups that the right question at the right time was the best way to unlock metacognitive insights which could move pupils' learning on. Questions posed when pupils are stuck or have just made a breakthrough could be well chosen to help to elicit wisdom from the team or capture metacognitive experiences. This process of asking the right (simple and well-chosen) question at the right moment appears to me to be the most powerful tool in this process. This can only be achieved with careful attunement to individual and team processes. For instance, in my experience pupils who are frustrated, angry, over-excited or nervous tend not to be receptive to this form of questioning. Similarly, successful metacognitive questioning is dependent on a high-quality relationship between the pupil and teacher. My experience suggests that the nature of this relationship can vary, however, it is imperative that the relationship is learning-focused and there are clear boundaries in place so that the pupil has clarity over the teacher's expectations and purpose.

A third and final significant feature of this attunement is the ability of the supporting adult to match the metacognitive question to the existing or emerging thoughts and feelings of the pupil or group. For instance, a pupil who is beginning to show some level of discomfort about a task might be helped by being asked the question, 'How are you feeling about this task?' or 'How might having a go at this task affect you?' A pupil who is struggling to find a way forward on a task but is clearly interested in doing so is likely to benefit from questions such as, 'What do you know already? What do we need to find out?' A pupil who proposes an answer that they themselves are somewhat surprised by is likely to benefit from being asked, 'How do you know?' My point here is that I have not found these questions to reap rewards when pupils are not receptive to them. A child who is disengaged or simply not 'on the same page' as you is likely to perceive these questions as alien and threatening. Paying attention to the extent to which pupils are ready to reflect on their learning and thinking is crucial, as is making the question relevant to their current situation.

In order to engage individuals, small groups or whole classes in these sorts of metacognitive enquiries, pupils need to be engaged in well-structured, well-pitched and well-understood tasks in well-managed classes. I believe that getting these elements in place is fundamental to being able to engage pupils in metacognitive thought about these tasks and in these contexts.

Verb-ing a verb

Having trained to teach in a manner informed by the work of Bloom (1956), I was accustomed to planning lessons with a learning objective that consisted of a verb acting on a noun, e.g. I can evaluate (verb) the actions of Jesus in Holy Week (noun). On this project, I felt the pressure to design RE lessons to facilitate metacognition – a shift in thinking onto the thinking/learning process itself. My solution was to incorporate one learning objective into another one, so that one thinking skill was being actively applied to one's performance at another task, e.g. I can explain (verb) how I evaluate (verb) the actions of Jesus in Holy Week (noun). A summary of such a lesson follows:

Activity 6: How good is that?

Lesson objective: I can *compare* how I *evaluate* different types of religious artefact

This lesson was designed to be used early on in a unit of work on Hinduism. The lesson engaged pupils with three dissimilar elements of the Hindu faith which are all significant to Hindus but for different reasons. Thus, this task introduces pupils to a range of ways in which Hinduism manifests itself in objects. These can be experienced and accompanied by simple explanations of their usage and significance in Hindu communities. The artefacts were available from the resources zone. The children were challenged to answer a question for each object in the form: 'Is this a good religious *painting/piece of text/portion of food*, etc.?' The children were challenged to compare how they went about evaluating the different items. Initially pupils discussed the different means by which they experienced the artefacts, e.g. through taste, sight, reading, smell, etc. Pupils then considered the criteria by which they judged the artefacts, e.g. whether they were beautiful, made sense, were true, tasted good, were produced by a skilled artist, etc. This extended into a paired activity where the pupils placed cards naming the different artefacts' qualities (e.g. taste, beauty, colour, use, etc.) on a Venn diagram according to whether they were considered when each of the three artefacts was evaluated. Finally, the pupils considered whether we use different processes when evaluating how good items of different types are; whether the fact these items are religious makes a difference to the processes we use; and whether it would be appropriate to say that any of the items are better than the others.

This approach had its drawbacks. When mixing and matching verbs relating to thinking, the results were mixed. A lesson which required pupils to generate different ways to identify parts of a church may be a useful revision session, but done in this way, it began to produce lessons that were too obscure for some pupils. Furthermore, the subject content was becoming lost in these kinds of inquiry into the nature of cognition. For example, a lesson evaluating different methods of recalling religious stories made the religion element of it almost unnecessary. In some respects, this model created a form of critical thinking, which was a long way from the original purpose of the project. However, I did have success with this when I matched a lower order thinking skill with a higher one to lessen the cognitive demand. The idea of a verb acting on a verb has proved to be a useful tool for me when generating questions. E.g. Can you *explain* to me how you have *summarised* this parable?

Don't underestimate the subject

I began this project working on the assumption that, generally speaking, RE lessons do not 'stimulate and demand a lot of careful, highly conscious thinking'. That they do not 'provide novel situations, where every major step you take requires planning beforehand and evaluation afterwards, where decisions and actions are at once weighty and risky'. That they do not 'provide an environment where high affective arousal and other inhibitors of reflective thinking are absent' (Flavell, 1979, p. 908). That learning about religion(s) and worldview(s) was not sufficiently important to most children to trigger metacognitive experiences. However, as the project progressed, I wondered whether we could foster in our pupils a real interest in the learning process and themselves as RE learners. As such, I have explored lesson ideas where the inquiry question is along the lines of, 'How well does … help us understand … ?' Following is an example of one such lesson:

Activity 7: 'Submission impossible?'– Exploring the viability of understanding submission to Allah

This lesson was designed to open or extend a unit of work introducing Year 5 pupils to Islam. The lesson was designed to familiarise pupils with the Five Pillars of Islam, but also, more significantly, to open up the question of what it would mean to understand submission to Allah. The pupils were given the opportunity to evaluate a fictional teacher's planning. They were told that the teacher had planned a series of activities to show children what it means for a Muslim to submit to Allah.

The hypothesis I held was that children from a non-Islamic background would recognise that none of the activities in the lesson would suffice as a means of understanding submission to Allah, and that children from Islamic backgrounds might also witness the remoteness of these classroom-based activities compared to their lived experience. For this lesson, I organised a rotation of six learning activities (one for each pillar of Islam plus another on the topic of submission) for the children to evaluate their usefulness.

Station 1: Pupils to copy out a definition of submission on paper and decorate with Islamic images and calligraphy.

Station 2: Pupils to decode a code which, when decoded, revealed the central statement of faith (the Shahadah): 'There is no god except Allah, and Muhammad is the messenger of Allah'.

Station 3: Pupils were required to follow and learn step-by-step instructions to performing whole-body prayer movements associated with Salat.

Station 4: Pupils work out 3% of given incomes so that they can consider how much Muslims are required to give to charity as part of their 'almsgiving' (Zakat).

Station 5: Pupils resist eating a pile of cookies in the centre of the table and imagine how Muslims might feel when they are fasting (Sawm).

Station 6: Pupils watch a short video on the Hajj and make notes on what the Hajj entails.

This lesson was designed to prompt valuable methodological discussions about what activities would have been a more effective means of meeting this lesson objective and to evaluate whether this is what we should be trying to do in RE. Furthermore, philosophical discussions can arise about the extent to which it is possible to 'know' another person's experience.

Conclusion

Over the course of the project I realised that metacognition in relation to RE was particularly valuable when it exposed deep questions for pupils about four main themes:

- The nature of truth
- The nature of religion(s) and worldview(s)
- The pupils' receptivity to learning about religion(s) and worldview(s)
- The nature of the study of religion(s) and worldview(s)

This has enhanced my practice as a Specialist Leader of Education. Now I seize opportunities when delivering the curriculum to engage pupils in philosophical discussion of the nature of truth: asking metacognitive questions such as, 'How do you know that this is true?', I no longer shy away from the complexity surrounding the nature of religion(s) and worldview(s): asking pupils to consider what type of subject matter they are being asked to engage with. Pupils in my classes are invited to share their feelings about the tasks set and to speculate as to why they feel the way they do about them.

Finally, I have begun to deconstruct and co-construct our class inquiries into religions and worldviews by inviting pupils to consider the nature of the tasks and questions set and to evaluate the success of different approaches to engaging with and learning about religion(s) and worldview(s). The pupils have welcomed the creation of a safe psychological space to engage with the subject matter whilst being invited to co-research answers to ultimate questions, religion(s) and worldview(s) and RE through motivating and meaningful tasks.

Further reading

Anderson L.W. and Krathwohl, D.R. (eds.). (2000) *A Taxonomy for Learning, Teaching and Assessing*. Essex, UK: Pearson.

Freathy, G., Freathy, R., Doney, J., Walshe, K. and Teece, G. (2015) *The RE-searchers: A New Approach to Primary Religious Education*. Exeter, UK: University of Exeter.

Taylor, T. (2016) *A Beginner's Guide to Mantle of the Expert: A Transformational Approach to Education*. London: Singular Publishing.

Teacher voice 3
A teacher's view of using the lessons (Cari)

Like most teachers, I was very happy to be given some planning, especially some planning that made teaching RE interesting and more interactive for children, as this is not always the case when following a local syllabus.

The Easter 'Throne together' plan was very useful and tackled an area of the Easter subject which is often glossed over in class – indeed, Easter is the festival which is a source of dread to most teachers precisely because it is so overlaid with spiritual and personal understanding and emotions. Most of us prefer not to get too deeply into it with primary age children and instead concentrate on how Easter is celebrated. By asking the pupils to look at the meaning of kingship, we were able to approach the story from a different path, one which led us through our understanding of power, salvation and leadership. The Year 6 class I worked with were mainly atheist and quite vocal. There were one or two practising Christians and a few declared Wiccans, Buddhists and agnostics.

I asked six children who are often excluded from groups and work very badly together to choose a team each based on the people they thought would perform the task well together (in all but one case, they chose really well, gathering people round them for their different skills). I gave them the storyline (there were some problems here, as a few wanted to have an armed coup against the grasshoppers and not wait for a saviour at all!). There was some surprise when I emptied two bags of assorted textiles, etc. onto the floor and gave them a chair to turn into a throne. I asked them their thoughts as they began the task. Most were quite excited, making comments such as, 'This is not like our usual RE', 'Do we have to design it?', 'What sort of throne?' and even 'Is it like a competition for the best design?' To avoid a rush for the resources, I asked them to nominate someone to fetch them for the group; they would be allowed to go back and swap pieces if they changed their minds. The building process went without any problems and the groups worked well. The designs were (predictably) shiny, gaudy and 'royal', one or two had incorporated crowns or weapons –

I asked, 'Why have you chosen those materials?' The answers were generally about what a throne usually looks like or the quality of the fabric (soft, comfortable, protective, sparkly). I asked – 'How do you know what sort of throne a king would want?' – again, the answers mainly began, 'Kings live in palaces/they are rich/they have armies/they are grand or posh' – 'All kings?' – at this point there was some hesitation – perhaps in other countries where they are not so rich it would be different.

When they finished, we took photographs and each group was invited to talk about how they worked together and whether they had learnt anything from the task. We stored the thrones and I told them the coming King would look at their designs and choose one – a week later I broke the bad news that he had rejected all of them! There was outrage.

The discussion around why the king would reject them revealed that the children all felt THEY had not done a good enough job. Eventually, we got to the idea that maybe their thrones were fine for the sort of king they had in mind, but perhaps there was more than one kind of king. This led to a discussion about the qualities we would want in a king – and eventually to the servant king. At this point, one of the Christian children clicked and stood up to give a very moving testament to his own beliefs about Jesus as King and the meaning of Easter. It was a natural conclusion to the lesson – not prompted or rehearsed, and his statement of belief was accepted as just that.

This is what I have realised:

Defining 'metacognition' is hard and often confused with 'critical thinking'.
It takes time to build a shared vocabulary, and thrashing out the difference between 'know' and 'believe', for instance, can become a whole lesson in itself, time which is not always available in a crowded curriculum.
Children need to be 'trained' to stop and consider how they are learning, what is influencing their ideas, how they feel about the task/learning, etc. and to use precise vocabulary to explain; metacognition needs to be embedded in the lessons.
Some children find the questioning uncomfortable and want to give the right answer or do not have the language to express what they feel or think and resort to 'dunno'.
Doing is powerful – the creative act leads to participation, and peer questioning elicits some great thinking – as a teacher our job shifts from telling to listening and occasionally prompting.
Creating an atmosphere where children take control of their own learning and respect each other's beliefs is very powerful.
All children have ideas about the meaning of life, but they are not often asked to talk about them.

The project and assessment 6

This chapter provides an insight into how the RE-flect project changed the teachers' views of teaching in RE. It begins with contextual information about the types of schools involved and what teachers initially said about the teaching of RE in their schools. The chapter provides a realistic view of how RE is often viewed in schools and the types of activities provided for primary school children. It goes on to show what teachers on the project subsequently came to believe about the opportunities RE can provide to develop children's thinking and the various ways in which the project has impacted on their classrooms. The chapter then focuses on the difficult and complex issue of assessment in RE. This is discussed in relation to wider issues of assessment and links to policy changes over time. Drawing on observational data from the RE-flect project, we discuss the reality of assessment in RE and show how such an assessment might be improved. Finally, a description is given of the types of assessment used in the project; the strengths and challenges of these; and what the data subsequently told us about the impact of the RE-flect project on children's learning and perception of RE.

The RE-flect schools and their RE lessons

Primary schools in the South West of England were approached via the University's PGCE Partnership Office and through links with the local authority advisor for RE. Initially, the focus was on recruiting fully maintained non-faith primary schools with a Year 5 class of at least 20 pupils (the reasons for focusing on Year 5 classes have been set out in the Introduction). However, perhaps not surprisingly, voluntary aided Church of England schools also applied to take part, and some rural schools had fewer than 20 pupils. Due to the collaborative nature of the project, we aimed to work with no more than ten schools. Seven schools took part in the pilot year of the project, with six of these continuing into the second year.

The schools were representative of a variety of settings, some being the only school serving a village community, whilst others were in rural towns or on the edge of larger conurbations. The nature of the area is such that there is relatively little ethnic diversity within the schools and a tendency to have fairly high levels of socio-economic disparity; a number of the schools had higher than average numbers of pupil premium attendees. (The pupil premium is additional funding for publicly funded schools in England to raise the attainment of disadvantaged pupils of all abilities and to close the gaps between them and their peers).

School A was a medium-sized primary school serving a small rural village. The buildings were a mixture of old and new, with the room in which the project teaching took place being in the oldest part of the school, in a small but light Victorian part of the building. The teacher was employed on a part-time basis, teaching RE to different classes, in different classrooms, across the school, usually when the class teacher was involved in PPA time. The peripatetic nature of this teacher's role, combined with the restricted space available in the classroom, made it very difficult to establish the specific zones.

School B was one of a number of primary schools in and around a small rural town. The buildings were relatively modern and spacious, with a large upstairs classroom used for the teaching of RE. The space allowed for significant room to be devoted to the worldview and meta-thinking zones, and the resource zone included a variety of artefacts relating to the current topic. The teacher was not the main class teacher but taught the group for RE as well as art and design. The teacher was redeployed from Year 5 at the end of the first year but was keen to remain involved in the project in the second year, where she worked with a Year 3 class (7–8-year-olds).

School C was a larger than average community primary school set in a village just a few miles from the centre of a city. It differed from the other schools in the project in that it was deemed a 'flagship' school for technology. With the exception of children in Reception, each child had their own computer to work on, which they used almost exclusively. Group work was limited by the layout of the classroom (computers are laid out in a three-way linear arrangement), meaning that each pupil can only practically work with their neighbour on each side – thus limiting groups to a maximum of three. Whilst the teacher was able to allocate space for a meta-thinking zone, the worldview zone was entirely a virtual space, with children working directly on their Worldview Profiles through the computer system using electronic documents.

School D was a Voluntary Controlled Church of England school, with an explicitly Christian ethos, and served as the main primary school in a small rural village. It had relatively new buildings, with light and airy classroom spaces. The teacher we worked with in this school took responsibility for RE across a number of classes.

School E was a larger-than-average primary school on the edge of a city; it had a strong Christian ethos, being a Voluntary Aided Church of England School. The classroom was light and airy, with a dedicated area for the resources zone, which included books and artefacts and had beanbags for pupils to sit on whilst they used the zone. Due to changes in employment, the teacher was only involved for the first year of the project.

School F was a larger-than-average primary school set in a rural town. The buildings were spacious, and the classroom of the teacher we worked with was light and spacious, with a number of different types of displays adorning the walls. Here the teacher took an innovative approach to the meta-thinking zone, using laminated cards on tables.

School G was a Church of England primary school of above-average size, with a strong Christian ethos. It served a large village situated between two urban areas. The buildings were recent, providing relatively spacious, well-lit classrooms. The teacher made space for all three zones.

At the start of the project, we gathered information about the way that RE was being taught and experienced in each of the schools. Each of our partner teachers completed a questionnaire about the nature of RE in their school, each contributed to a group discussion with the research team during the first of the teacher days and each participated in a one-to-one interview with the research assistant. From these activities, we were able to see at the start of the project that, whilst all of the schools were supposed to be teaching RE according to their respective Local Education Authority's Agreed Syllabus for RE, none of them were. Provision was often sporadic, sometimes changed at the last moment due to other curriculum demands, and when they did occur, RE lessons often focused on ethical and environmental issues or were devoted to creative artistic activities.

Overall, we think it is fair to say that for our project schools, RE was given a low status and seen as a low priority, often being passed on from the main class teacher to others. At the start of the project, some of the teachers mentioned a lack of confidence in their subject knowledge in relation to their perceptions that the subject was important,

> It just wasn't something that I was interested in, it wasn't something that I had a background knowledge in, and I suppose I was scared of getting it wrong. And it's quite an important [subject] … I valued it enough to not do it and get it wrong, because I thought that if I'm providing misconceptions about religion, that would be worse than doing nothing.
>
> (Teacher, School A)

Some of the teachers had, and continued to wrestle with, questions of just who is an appropriate person to teach RE, asking whether as 'a non-religious person' it was appropriate to share personal views with the pupils. In terms of the lessons that were taking place, there were many examples that showed that there was a relatively superficial engagement with religion(s), often through a reliance on brought-in artefacts and basic information sharing. As one teacher said,

> It would be these festivals exist, this is how they keep these festivals, this is food that might be eaten at a festival, it was very much an onlooker's guide, from a distance that this is what one might see if you were watching a Hindu wedding or a Muslim wedding, but it wouldn't be anything about the values or beliefs.
>
> (Teacher, School A)

In addition to our conversations with teachers throughout the project, interviews with pupils were also undertaken. Six pupils from each class involved in the project were interviewed, in fixed boy/girl pairs, at the start and end of each academic year. The same questions were posed each time; these concentrated on ascertaining the pupils' attitudes towards and interest in RE, as well as particular classroom practices that their teachers were using.

These interviews revealed that pupils had a mixed reaction to the type of RE that had been going on when the project began, with some pupils reporting that they found these sorts of RE lessons boring and had little understanding of the content of recent lessons. After a lesson focusing on stories of the Buddha, one pupil could only recall that, 'We've started doing about, err … learn about a story sort of and just listen to a story' (Billy).

> What do you think are the characteristics of your current RE lessons?

Other pupils clearly found the lessons more valuable, 'I like learning about other religions, because it's nice to know what happens in other people's lives, not just ours' (Cerys). However, confusion over the nature and purpose of RE lessons was clear. In response to the question, 'What have you been doing in RE lately?', one pupil responded: 'Err, we've been doing about Romans and all different kinds of stuff like … err … our now topic is musical instruments' (Amy). There seems to be a confusion in her mind between RE lessons and other lessons.

> How would your pupils describe your RE lessons? How do you know that this is how they see them?

The lack of opportunity for discussion was raised; some pupils reflecting that RE lessons comprised 'just sitting in the classroom, listening to the teacher' (Cerys), whilst others offered a suggestion for change, '[we'd like] more like talking time, because usually we don't really have much discuss time, all we do is like Miss tells us what to do and then we just go off and we work by ourself' (Amy).

The difference the project made

At the end of the project, when they were interviewed again, teachers recounted that their perceptions of, and their practices of RE, were very different. Enthusiasm for the subject had changed, with one teacher commenting,

> I love RE, I feel that I am actually giving something of myself to the children and benefiting them. They're getting probably better, especially Year 5 RE lessons, and I find it is constructive because they have improved. And I am taking that from Year 5 to Year 4 and Year 6. And so I think it is constructive, because it's building … they are beginning to think a bit deeper.
>
> (Teacher, School D)

Another reported:

> I didn't have any starting points. Now, I've started seeing that one can question different religions and ask your own questions of it. So what does it mean to me or how does this or that faith affect me, what's it got to do with me? So religion isn't being done to you, it's you trying to put yourself in a position where you can make an informed opinion of a religion and how people might feel about being Hindu, Muslim, Jewish, and questions that could be asked of people who have that faith.
>
> (Teacher, School A)

At the time of the project, non-statutory guidance for RE set out two attainment targets for the subject, Learning about Religions and Learning From Religion (Qualifications & Curriculum Authority [QCA], 2004). The idea of 'learning from religion' was considered one of the most difficult aspects of teaching RE. Certainly, our experience from the project was that this was the case. However, we also found, in the teacher interviews and in some of the other feedback from the teachers at the end of the project, that there was now a more sophisticated understanding of 'learning from religion'.

In terms of their approach to RE, one teacher said,

> I think my approach to RE teaching is different and there is – even though that's quite important for me – less of a focus on subject knowledge and being able to name every single festival type thing. I think that's what it's helped me with, thinking about you don't have to do that, you can look at RE from a different way, it doesn't have to be knowledge-based. I think that approach and looking at what they already know and drawing out what they already know and sharing ideas, is something that I'll take to other subjects, which will be good.
>
> (Teacher, School C)

By creating metacognitive environments in which their RE lessons took place, teachers reported that they felt that they had more freedom in their lessons, with less focus on literacy and 'an end product'. The way that questioning was used had changed, there was a stronger emphasis on the sources of beliefs and knowledge and the pace of lessons had slowed. This change led to changes in the nature of classroom activities,

> Well, before it was just a simple research exercise; you need to find out about festivals of light, find out about them. But now ... it's asking ... what relation on people's lives do these have? Does it have any bearing on my life? Am I involved in any of these festivals? Do I know of anybody else who's involved in these festivals? So it's ... wanting to know more for yourself. It's the "I wonders", I suppose ... as in you can help people develop their curiosity and willingness to know more about it, but you can't make them curious.
>
> (Teacher, School A)

Moreover, the role played by pupils in the classroom had changed, with pupils taking a more active role in their own learning, evident through them leading discussion (rather than responding to teacher-initiated discussion) and demonstrating developing group discussion skills, with pupils asking more questions and making connections between what they were learning,

> They are very willing now to … talk and share their ideas and perhaps understand … not all of them; a lot of them, to understand how listening to each other perhaps means their ideas change. We had a discussion the other day and it was different scenarios of things that could happen, things like you find a bag of money in the street in a black bag, what do you do with it? And we had various discussions, they discussed it in groups and things like that, and then we had feedback about what they were saying. And some children put their hands up initially and said, "oh, I would take the money, because these people are hopeless …" and then listening to some of the other comments and the explanations, go back to them and go, "actually, no, I think that this might be a better idea". So that kind of listening to each other's been quite good. And perhaps to a certain extent being able to explain why they got to that answer. Not always. Not always. But they can, I think, explain more about how they got there.
> (Teacher, School C)

Some teachers described how involvement in the project had affected their own thinking, 'I think I've begun to see reflection as quite a positive thing to do, rather than that kind of dreadful, quasi-psychological self-analysis that some of us go in for' (Teacher, School B). Further, they reported that their pupils became more interested in 'Big Questions', were more motivated, were enjoying RE more and, ultimately, learnt more.

In their later interviews, pupils also commented on changes in their experience of RE, with a greater degree of clarity over the content of their RE lessons than had been the case at the start of the project, 'We learn about different faiths and what they do in them. So who they worship and what their everyday life is like' (Lizzie, School A), with a generally more positive attitude towards RE lessons, 'They're like … fun … good fun' (Freddie, School A). The sense of challenge was voiced alongside this,

> sometimes RE really makes you think. Well, Miss B gives you hard work, so it really makes you think on are you going [to] put this or are you going to put that. And then you're thinking, and then Miss B tells you to get on with it, so you just like have to have one sentence or another.
> (George, School B)

Some pupils actively sought to be stretched in this way; one reported,

> I generally like [RE lessons] when they're not something that you already know, so not something very easy, and if they're not too … really, really, deeply religious. If you tell me the Christmas Story again and again and again that will be a bit boring, but if you told me something slightly more new about the Christmas Story I might be a bit more interested.
> (Beatrix, School C)

In addition to these interviews with teachers and with pupils, a questionnaire was used to examine the impact of creating metacognitively oriented RE classrooms on participating pupils' perceptions of their learning environment. The Religious Education Metacognitive Orientation Scale (REMOS) was adapted from a general metacognitive orientation scale (GSMOS) created by Thomas and Mee (2005). It was used at the start and end of each academic year in the project. The scale has 15 statements (such as Q1: 'The teacher asks us to think about how we learn in Religious Education'; Q3: 'The teacher tells us how *she* thinks when *she* learns in Religious Education'). Pupils were asked to respond to each question using a three-point scale (Always, Sometimes, Never). Higher scores were associated with more metacognitively orientated classroom environments.

Results from the REMOS questionnaire showed that in all of the schools, scores increased between the beginning and end of the main phase of the project, with the largest increase in School C. This suggests that the RE-flect project successfully created metacognitively orientated RE classrooms and led pupils to consider the learning environment more positively.

Responses to the Worldview Profiles

As set out in Chapter 3, information about how Worldview Profiles were used in the different schools was gathered, showing that there was a variety of practice when it came to implementation at a number of levels, including format, structure and the selection of stimulus questions.

They were commented on widely, by both teachers and pupils, in positive ways. One teacher said,

> I do like the idea of the worldview diaries, I think they've been really good. I think it helps the children encounter things that they perhaps wouldn't normally. Nobody's ever asked them to tell anybody about their religious views, in fact some of them went "what are religious views?", but then nobody's ever asked them that question.
>
> (Teacher, School C)

Another teacher reported, 'I like the Worldview Profile, [thinking about] the wider world, and not just thinking about themselves. It is making them aware perhaps of other faiths' (Teacher, School D).

The degree of privacy afforded to the pupils was a key issue. This was most clearly manifested in the issue of whether feedback should be provided, something that had been a focus of discussion between the teachers and the research team. Whilst no firm recommendations were made, the potential lack of pupil engagement was considered. As a consequence of the decision by teachers to not provide feedback, in several cases, Worldview Profile entries evidenced a degree of confusion regarding the given task, which remained unaddressed by the teacher. Tina (School C), for example, responded to the question, 'Do you think the world had a beginning?' with 'I don't understand this question', while Jessica (School F) did not understand what was meant by 'non-physical things'. Additionally, George (School G) had no reason to question the compatibility of his two views that 'all people are equal' and 'some people are more important than others'.

The teachers' evaluations of the approach, and the extent to which the Worldview Profiles achieved their aims, were almost wholly positive. Teachers agreed (or strongly agreed) that the Worldview Profiles offered pupils the opportunity 'to communicate and justify their own ideas in relation to questions of identity and belonging, meaning, purpose and truth, and values and commitments' and 'to discuss and give reasons for their own and others' views of religious truth and belief, of life and its origin, purpose and meaning, and so on'. One teacher additionally commented that she strongly believed that Worldview Profiles offered opportunities for pupils to be able to answer questions with thoughtful answers, and another commented that she strongly believed that Worldview Profiles offered opportunities for pupils to become more aware of where their views originate, i.e. who influences them.

Whilst these results, and the oral feedback we received from teachers at other points, were very supportive of the worldview profiling approach, they confirm our earlier finding that opportunities were not provided to enable pupils to reflect upon the relationship between their Worldview Profiles and RE subject content and learning processes, particularly in terms of how their worldviews influence their conceptualisation of, and engagement with, RE curriculum content. The teachers' enthusiasm for the approach was possibly more orientated towards its general educational benefits than its contribution to initiating pupils into the communities of academic inquiry concerned with the study of religion(s) and worldview(s), such as through theological, religious and related studies.

Feedback from the teachers' questionnaires also suggests that the activities undertaken by pupils as part of Worldview Profiles were stimulating and engaging, with 80% of teachers agreeing that Worldview Profiles offered opportunities for pupils to express and communicate their own and others' insights through art and design, music, dance, drama and/or ICT. However, one teacher who agreed with this statement nonetheless additionally indicated that she felt opportunities were offered in relation to art and design and ICT but not in relation to music, dance or drama. Such a comment, therefore, demonstrates that, while worldview profiling remains open to the development and implementation of creative activities, teachers are in need of further permission, encouragement and support in order for such ideas to be successfully implemented.

Pupil feedback on the Worldview Profiles was also positive. The opportunity to have a space for personal reflection was seen positively, 'we can like make it personal and special, because no-one else gets to see it apart from us … we really like the books'. However, the confidentiality of the Worldview Profiles raised issues for some pupils; one pupil stated, 'Some people have written silly things in it. I haven't, because I know that as we're doing this then people will be looking through it. Some people in the class have written who they love and stuff'.

Some pupils reflected positively on the fact that the Worldview Profiles required them to have no religious knowledge, for example, one girl said,

> Well, we've got these books which we call our Worldview Profiles and the questions, they're not really about Buddhism and all that, so it's not like a test when they're saying who became the Buddha, A, B or C … That's a good thing.

Other pupils also noted the emphasis being placed upon the learning process rather than the provision of an approved product: a boy stated, 'So she doesn't tell us what the answer is, she just tells us how to work it out basically … Sort of like in maths'. Another boy from the same school said, 'Well, at the start we normally do hard questions that we have to answer in our world profile books, and then we go into some normal activities'. By contrast, and perhaps indicating the diversity of approaches across the different schools or maybe just the diversity of pupil responses, a boy from another school indicated, 'I haven't used mine that much, I just normally draw pictures in them'.

There was some limited evidence that the pupils had recognised that their responses to questions had changed. One stated,

> Some of the things I've done, like I write down some of the things because that's what I feel like then, but some of the things I've changed a bit … It's like I go back to that page and change what I wrote.

Similarly, there was also some limited evidence that the pupils recognised the relationship between their Worldview Profiles and the worldviews of others,

> So the Worldview Profiles, because we've got books for it, so we can have like lots of stuff put in … err … and do something like that question, what do you believe, and then also like … think about … then you could like have a bit that links on about what others believe, because that would link into it.

Some of the pupil responses indicated that the worldview profiling approach might have become formulaic. By the end of the year, one pupil described the approach simply as follows, 'Well, we usually write the answer to the question, how we feel, and then we do a picture. If it was asking you about Poppy Day you'd like draw a poppy with like a cross'. Another complained,

> We sort of do them [the Worldview Profiles] generally for the beginning, while she sets up, like just answering the questions. Which I find quite boring really … It was good at the beginning, because you just got some questions, they're interesting questions, but it's like if you did them over and over … and it's like it doesn't matter because it's your thing.

This may indicate a bigger issue around what pupils value in terms of their own learning. Rather than focusing on thinking more deeply about the questions and reflecting on them further, this pupil's answer suggests that the focus is on receiving a mark or some acknowledgement by the teacher. We would hope that rather than 'it's your thing' being a reason for it not mattering, 'it's your thing' would come to be seen as crucial to learning in RE and to education more generally.

In hindsight, the RE-flect project team could have provided clearer instructions, model activities, undertaken more collaborative lesson planning and/or developed units of work to demonstrate how the Worldview Question Framework and worldview profiling might be creatively applied in lessons, utilising a diversity of content, methods and lesson structures. Additional input was provided by the consultant teacher primarily with regard to the meta-thinking zone, but clearly more advice and guidance was needed in relation to the worldview zone too. Such provision may have increased the confidence of our teacher collaborators and inspired them to be more inventive in the design of new teaching and learning activities to support worldview profiling. This would have been particularly beneficial in terms of helping teachers tackle the issue of differentiation.

Assessment and the project

Assessment in RE is a complex and complicated issue, yet the matter has received comparatively less attention from researchers than curriculum development and pedagogy (Fancourt, 2010 and 2014). At the time of the RE-flect project, a standardized eight-point scale, based on the two Attainment Targets (AT1 and AT2) discussed earlier, through which pupil progress should be monitored, had been developed by the RE community (see, for example, QCA, 2004), which was taken up in many locally Agreed Syllabuses for RE. Some criticisms of the levels have been consistent, including the fact that progress through the levels is not sequential. For example, Level 1 requires skills of 'recollecting and expressing', whilst Level 2 focuses on 'identifying and questioning'.

Ofsted (Office for Standards in Education) considers assessment in RE as 'a major weakness in the schools visited. It was inadequate in a fifth of the secondary schools and a third of the primary schools. Many teachers were confused about how to judge how well pupils were doing in RE' (Office for Standards in Education, 2013, p. 6). The extent to which this is related to the use, or non-use, of the eight-level scale is unclear. However, we found that at the start of our project, none of the participating teachers were using this scale, and many were unaware of it altogether.

Work undertaken by the Religious Education Council (REC) suggests that the lack of knowledge about the criteria and lack of use of the eight-point scale was not peculiar to our teachers (Blaylock et al., 2013). There seems to be a wider lack of understanding of the nature and purpose of RE across primary RE classrooms, even where teachers are working from the same locally Agreed Syllabus.

In 2014, a policy announcement was made that 'the current system of "levels" used to report children's attainment and progress will be removed. It will not be replaced' (DFE, 2014, p. 2). Since this announcement, schools have been encouraged to develop their own approach to assessment in National Curriculum subjects, which has led to a wide variety of practices being adopted and developed, including those centred on Bloom's Taxonomy, SOLO grids and Mastery approaches. A Research Report published by the National College for Teaching & Leadership (Lilly, Peacock, Shoveller and Struthers, 2014) reported that schools have adopted a variety of responses to the challenge of assessment 'after levels', although these responses are sometimes inconsistent both within and across schools. Whilst the report made recommendations regarding the purpose of assessment, the use of technology for tracking assessment data and support for collaborative development of new assessment approaches, no concrete recommendations about the nature of such approaches were made.

One consequence of the changing nature and purpose of assessment is an expanding interest in self-assessment in RE, recognising that although more widely used, the area is also under-researched (Fancourt, 2010). Nigel Fancourt (2005) suggests that self-assessment in RE can be broken down into four areas (Self-assessment *of* learning *about* religions; Self-assessment *for* learning *about* religions; Self-assessment *of* learning *from* religion; Self-assessment *for* learning *from* religion). He notes that the third and fourth can be problematic, particularly in terms of possible confusion between 'self-assessment' and 'learning from religions'. With regard to the first area, approaches such as quizzes or extended writing tasks (where assessment criteria are clear and communicated to pupils in ways that enable their understanding) can be useful in helping pupils understand what they have learned and understood. The second area focuses more on what the pupil knows in relation to what they might explore next. Questions such as 'I already know... ; I would like to find out ... ; I need to know more about ... ; I would like to improve ... ' (Copley and Priestley, 1991, p. 140). To these four areas, we would add a fifth: the area of self-assessment of metacognition, as discussed in Chapter 1.

> How do you assess your pupils in RE? What changes to assessment would you like to see?

In order to evaluate the effect of developing metacognitive environments on pupils' attainment, we created a 12-point scale for teachers to evaluate learning in RE at pre- and post-project points. This scale kept the AT1 and AT2 attainment targets and was based on the eight-level national scale, but allowed for greater discrimination in assessment by effectively introducing sub-targets, a practice that was commonly used in other National Curriculum assessments prior to the 2013 policy change. This subdivision was based in our case on the degree to which a piece of work fitted the given criteria. For example, we took the level descriptor for AT1 at level 2,

> Pupils use religious words and phrases to identify some features of religion and its importance for some people. They begin to show awareness of similarities in religions. Pupils retell religious stories and suggest meanings for religious actions and symbols. They identify how religion is expressed in different ways.
>
> (QCA, 2004, p. 36)

and the corresponding AT2 level descriptor at the same level,

> Pupils ask, and respond sensitively to, questions about their own and others' experiences and feelings. They recognise that some questions cause people to wonder and are difficult to answer. In relation to matters of right and wrong, they recognise their own values and those of others.
>
> (QCA, 2004, p. 36)

Then we asked teachers to consider their pupils' work using these descriptors. If they saw signs that 1 or 2 of these things were present and they were thinking, 'sometimes they do this', that would be a Low Level 2. If at least half of the criteria were met, then it would be graded as a Mid Level 2, and if all of them were clearly present, a High Level 2.

At the start of the academic year, we asked our teachers to grade a piece of current work using this process and award a level on our 12-point scale. In order to have confidence in this measure, we supported teachers through the provision of information and instruction on how to assess AT1 and AT2. This was moderated by a member of the research team comparing different examples of pupil work awarded the same grade by the class teacher. The grades were then compared across the participating schools to ensure parity. We also asked teachers to predict an attainment level for each pupil for the end of the year. At the end of the school year, teachers graded another piece of work using our 12-point scale, and we compared the teacher's predicted grade with the end of year grade for each pupil in each of the classes.

The results show that we can claim some positive impact on attainment in RE for all except one school, although the improvement over predicted scores is relatively small. Overall, pupils did tend to do better than their teachers had predicted both in regard to 'learning about religions' (AT1) and 'learning from religion' (AT2) in two schools (Schools B and G), and in one or other of the targets in two other schools (Schools A and C). However, the claim needs to be treated with caution; the project did not follow a full experimental design, thus there were no control schools for comparison. Whilst there was some evidence of improved attainment, this was not the main focus of the project.

Conclusion

This chapter has shown how the RE-flect project changed the teachers' views of teaching in RE and pupils' experience of learning in RE. Whilst initially the teachers were unaware of the non-statutory national guidance that exists for RE, particularly in terms of assessment, by the end of the project teachers were much more confident about applying assessment criteria and working within the national guidance available at the time. Through interviews with teachers and pupils, we gained a picture of how RE is often viewed in primary schools and how these views might be positively impacted upon by creating a metacognitive learning environment. The project teachers and pupils became more positive about RE and its possibilities for deeper self-reflection. We also found an increase in levels of attainment in RE in most of the schools involved.

Further reading

Blaylock, L., Gent, B., Stern, J. and Walshe, K. (2013) *Subject Review of Religious Education in England, Phase 1: Report of the Expert Panel*. London: Religious Education Council.

Fancourt, N. (2005) 'Challenges for Self-assessment in Religious Education'. *British Journal of Religious Education*, 27 (2), 115–125.

Lilly, J., Peacock, A., Shoveller, S. and Struthers, d'R. (2014) *Beyond Levels: Alternative Assessment Approaches Developed by Teaching Schools; Research Report*. Nottingham, UK: National College for Teaching and Leadership.

Teacher voice 4
Teachers' views of being involved in the RE-flect project

During the project, we ran three teacher days where our project teachers came together to discuss their experiences of putting the project into practice. Here we present some of the experiences and thoughts related to us during these teacher days. The quotations represent how individual teachers felt, but they were often supported by similar experiences from others in the group. Thus, rather than name individuals in this section, we present quotations which represent a spectrum of comments by all the RE-flect project teachers.

Impact of the project

> At first I found it quite hard to get them to answer anything. But now I have to put a time limit on it. So the other day they were answering one of the big questions about why we learn RE in school. They had to write their own answer and the whole room was quiet and they were scribbling away. Some of them had written a whole side in five minutes and these included kids who hardly wrote anything before. If I'd have asked them this before they would just have said "because we have to".
>
> It's a different way of learning. I would say out of the 52 children I teach, 35 of them have definitely benefited from working in a more reflective, more open way. I think it will certainly benefit them in year 6. They are more articulate and they have more to say.

'At the beginning of the year they were reluctant to give their opinion because others would laugh, but now they are much more accepting of other people's views'.

> One little boy asked me, "Miss, what does heaven look like?", and all the others cracked up laughing and said, "doesn't he know, heaven is up in the clouds", so I said,

"hold on a minute, you are all laughing but this is the biggest question anyone has ever asked me and can we unpick this a little bit". So all the ones who had laughed had to step back a little bit and think about it and explore their own views and feelings about it. It took a real turn in the lesson.

Challenges and difficulties

I looked at the Worldview Profiles recently and I noticed that there were a lot of conflicting views in there. So they were saying, "I don't believe in a higher being" and then the next minute they were saying, "God created the world". So there was a lot of confusion. I wonder if that is because as a faith school they feel they have to give "the right answer".

'Visitors to the school, including faith groups, who come to tell stories or put on plays don't always make clear that they are operating from a particular faith point of view'.

I had difficulty with displays as they were taken down by the class teacher. It is heartbreaking to put all that work in and then find it all just put in a drawer somewhere. In the end we got some corridor space and I think that was good because the whole school could see the displays.

Pupils and teachers developing metacognition

7

In the previous chapter we described some general ways in which both pupils and teachers changed their attitudes towards RE, but how did those changes come about? In this chapter, we draw on video data from the classrooms to illustrate what we mean by metacognition in the RE context and how it might be manifested through group discussion and individual interaction with resources. We share some of the surprises and moments of insight we observed during the project, and we explore some of the tensions that teachers experienced. In the final part of the chapter, we show how teachers were encouraged to develop their own metacognition and how this impacted on their practice.

We collected one hour of classroom video observation per class per term, and the observations were focused on a group of six pupils per class. These pupils were followed throughout the year. We analysed these videos using a coding scheme based on Flavell's (1979) model of metacognition. We looked specifically for the categories of metacognition that featured in Flavell's original model (see Chapter 1), but in addition we also noted any elements of metacognition that were specific to this project, e.g. those focused specifically on aspects of RE. Tables 7.1–7.4 show the codes we used to categorize the data from the videos. These categories give some idea of the richness of the observation data we collected. We found examples of each category in the observations over the length of the project, with more examples observed later in the project. However, rather than focusing on the number of examples of each element of metacognition we observed, we were more interested in the quality of the interaction between the pupils and often surprising moments of revelation they displayed.

Have you observed a group of your pupils working together? Could you see a way to use the coding scheme referred to earlier?

We included cognitive as well as metacognitive strategies and knowledge, because in reality it can be very difficult to discern one from the other, and often the metacognitive

Table 7.1 Metacognitive strategy: Three categories – evaluation, monitoring and planning (C = Child/Children)

Evaluation	Monitoring
C evaluates own/group learning	C monitors group task
C evaluates a question	C challenges another's knowledge, thinking or belief
C evaluates own understanding of a religion	C discuss understanding
C evaluates own response to a task	C discuss source of beliefs
C evaluates collaborative working	
C has a positive/negative view of learning in RE	Planning
C checks with another C	C organises group task
	C takes lead in group work

Table 7.2 Metacognitive experiences: Four codes (C = Child/Children)

Metacognitive experience defined as –
brief or lengthy, simple or complex, sense of puzzlement; wonder if you understand; feel that you may fail or that you did well in a previous task; feel that you are not communicating how you feel; suddenly stuck on something; sense that something will be easy or difficult to understand, remember or solve; feeling that you are far from the cognitive goal (Flavell, 1979).

C expresses feeling of puzzlement	C expresses difficulty or being stuck	C refers to task as difficult (boring)	C expresses feelings about a religious image

Table 7.3 Metacognitive knowledge: 20 codes (C = Child/Children)

Self/Other/Universals of cognition

C expresses thinking related to self or community	C refers to source of knowledge
C expresses belief about the world	C refers to getting knowledge outside school
C refers to learning about self from RE	C refers to ways of getting knowledge in school
C links RE to believing	C refers to listening to learn
C refers to learning from RE	C refers to meta-thinking zone
C refers to social aspect of RE	C refers to worldview profiles
C expresses positive/negative view of learning in RE	C refers to classroom environment
C refers to gender differences in learning	C refers to process of learning in RE
C expresses view about a process of learning	C refers to repetition in learning in RE
C refers to progress in learning in RE	C refers to role play drama for learning in RE

Table 7.4 Cognitive strategies and knowledge: Ten codes (C = Child/Children, T = Teacher)

Cognitive strategies	Knowledge
C compares religions/worldviews	C expresses misunderstanding about a religion/worldviews
C repeats T questioning to another C	C refers to learning about religion/worldviews
C answers direct factual questions	C refers to learning about others
C co-construct a text	
C discuss and exchange ideas	
C justify their reasoning	
C acts out a scenario	

part of a dialogue came about from a cognitive process such as 'justifying reasoning'. At the moment, this probably feels quite abstract, so following we give an example of an interaction between pupils and then show how we applied the coding scheme mentioned earlier.

This is an extract from a lesson which focuses on the difference between 'know', 'believe', 'think' and 'wonder'. The groups each have one religious image which they have chosen themselves and which they are going to discuss using these words. This group has a very colourful image of a Sikh wedding, showing the bride and groom. (Pseudonyms are used for all the children).

Lisa: I believe that they have to wear turbans at every wedding.
Amy: I believe their turbans have to be the same colour as the dress.
Sam: I disagree.
Joe: I believe that they respect their religion.
Mia: But that's not to do with weddings.
Sam: I wonder why the girls don't wear dresses.
Joe: It's just what you believe, it doesn't have to be right. She might not be able to wear a dress.
Amy: Why don't we go around the table saying what we believe first and then say if we agree?

(They agree to do this, and a discussion follows on different aspects of the couple's dress. They come to a group decision that they 'wonder why the man's turban is red').

Amy: I believe it is because the turban has to be the same colour as the dress.
Joe: But if you believe that then you wouldn't wonder.
Amy: But I wonder as well sometimes.
Joe: It doesn't make sense; you said you believe they wear the same colour turban to match the woman's clothes and now you're saying I wonder why they do that.
Amy: Yeah but the thing is (clicks her fingers) oh everything is going out of my head. I've forgotten what I was going to say. Oh yeah, we believe he picked that turban to match her outfit but we wonder why he did that – is it just coincidence? What do you think, everyone?
Joe: I think he has to wear that sword to protect his wife.

At first sight, the exchange may appear to be of little consequence, but if we look at it more closely we see firstly that the whole group are engaged in talking about the image they have found and noticing things which may be of religious significance. Joe makes a first distinction when he says that belief does not have to be 'right', and he continues through the discussion to make similar distinctions. In this excerpt, it is Joe who highlights a seeming difference between belief and wonder. At this point, he is focusing on difference rather than on compatibility of the two terms. It is Amy, after expressing a cognitive conflict as she struggles to get her own thinking clear, who expresses the view that wonder can be linked to belief. At this stage, the group is focused on a concrete image, but it is possible to see how the teacher could build upon even this short interaction to highlight bigger, more abstract religious questions.

One of our most popular RE-flect lessons is the Easter-focused Sacrifice lesson (see Chapter 5), at the beginning of which children have to rate a number of different items before going on to play a trading game, sacrificing one item for another. In one school, the teacher began by doing a whole class Q&A asking which item is the most valuable: a watch, a mobile phone or a painting. The children were eager to give their opinion and their reasons, and there was obviously much disagreement. The teacher then began to focus on the disagreement.

Teacher: So why do you think we are having this disagreement about what is the most valuable?
Luca: Because some people are talking about how valuable it is to you but others are talking about how much money.
Ava: I valued it on how valuable they were to me. I didn't do it in a money way, so more like how your feelings are with them.

When the children go into groups, they each have 40 items to value and to discuss; one of these is 'your life' and another is 'the life of your only child'.

Charlie: I wouldn't really be bothered about my life because I wouldn't know about it, but my parents would be bothered, so I gave it six.

Charlie is demonstrating a metacognitive shift from thinking from his own point of view to thinking from the point of view of his parents.

Molly: I don't know how to rate the life of your only child.
Charlie: You have to imagine yourself as a grown-up.

Through the discussion, the group gets to know more about how everyone thinks and what everyone values. A group of three girls discuss the different values, ranging from one to eight to ten, that they attached to 'the life of your only child'. They were astonished to find such big differences between the way they thought about this item. This is another example of shifting their thinking from their own perspective to see and understand the perspective of others.

> Is there any time in your classroom when children learn about each other's values?

It is important with all the RE-flect activities that the link to RE is made clear. In this exchange the teacher does just that.

Teacher: So you have had a good discussion in your groups and you have given a rating to the items, but remember, this is an RE lesson, so what has all of this got to do with RE?
Oliver: Is it our personal beliefs?
Teacher: Yes, and does anyone remember anything about the Easter story?
Oliver: Somebody will betray Jesus and so he will die on the cross.
Teacher: Good, and what is the connection with what you have done today?
Ethan: The life of your child, because God gave his child to make the world a better place.

Ethan's statement seemed to come as a revelation to him and to the rest of the class, and it may not always be the case that the children can make the link for themselves. In this particular activity, the link may become clearer when they move to the next step and play the Ultimate Trading Game.

So far, metacognition has been displayed in terms of a developing theory of mind, i.e. in terms of understanding that other people have different beliefs, values and thoughts, even when looking at the same material or stimulus. Metacognition was also apparent in the groups in terms of group strategy for discussion. On a number of occasions, group discussion began to disintegrate until one member of the group halted proceedings and decided on a strategy such as taking turns to express views; one person writing notes while others talk; or otherwise organising the way in which the task would be done. Some teachers made a point of focusing on this aspect, getting groups to evaluate their own progress and rate their own group learning. Encouraging this type of group metacognition is important in building bridges between what happens in RE lessons and what happens in other lessons. Ultimately, we are aiming for the transfer of learning across subject domains, so that understanding self, others, tasks and goals becomes common practice and leads to more self-regulated learning.

Through the project, there were many occasions where pupils expressed puzzlement, frustration, disappointment and sometimes hostility towards the task. These can all be rewarding metacognitive experiences if they lead to some kind of insight. In the following exchange between three pupils, one of whom appears to be a confirmed atheist, they come to some understanding about how to talk about religion and faith.

To further protect anonymity, the pupils in this extract are referred to as C1, C2 and C3.

C1: Do you think I would get told off for saying I think it's pointless?
C2: What do you think it is?
C1: Pointless.
C2: What, Christians?
C1: Yeah.
C2: If you say it's rubbish you are breaking the law, but if you say it's pointless, I don't think you will get into trouble.
C3: It's not breaking the law saying it's rubbish, it's just a different view on it.
C1: Cos I do.
C2: You can say it's pointless as long as you don't offend anyone with it.

How can you encourage children in your class to express their ideas without fear?

They may not have fully resolved the issue of how to discuss religion and faith from a non-faith, or expressly anti-faith position, but by allowing C1 to express the view at all, we see some movement from fear of being castigated for holding the 'wrong' view to an acceptance by the group that people have a right to hold different views, albeit with some constraints. These types of exchanges happened when the children worked collaboratively in groups and had some freedom in how their group managed the task.

Teacher metacognition

Research on teacher metacognition has shown that developing metacognition helps with confidence and feelings of self-efficacy (Santisi, Magnano, Hichy and Ramaci, 2014). It enables teachers to find their own pedagogical solutions and to feel motivated to search for them (Portilho and Medina, 2016). In this sense, developing metacognition has much in common with the notion of the reflective practitioner, and often in the literature the focus is on teachers developing metacognition in order to improve their classroom practice. However, we took a slightly different approach to teacher metacognition, and rather than making an explicit link to practice, we encouraged teachers to focus on themselves; their own beliefs; and their own experiences of religion, faith, worldviews and RE. Thus, the fostering of metacognition was seen as for its own sake, a version of 'knowing oneself better', rather than for a pedagogical outcome.

To this end, we worked with an approach often used in counselling and psychotherapy. The approach was based on Kelly's (1955) personal construct theory. As its name suggests, this is a constructivist theory, i.e. we construct our knowledge and understanding of the world from how we interpret our own experiences of the world. Thus, it is not the experience itself which leads to knowledge and understanding but rather what we make of the experience. As we make meaning from all of our experiences we develop a theory of the way the world is, and that leads us to interpret present and future experiences through our own unique lens. Kelly referred to people as scientists testing our own theories against the evidence of our experiences and modifying our theory of the way the world is in light of new understandings. Thus, Kelly's theory is also dynamic. It is not that we adopt a single unified theory of the world in childhood and doggedly stick to that theory; instead, we are always engaged in a process of reflection and re-calculation. However, we can also become stuck in certain ways of thinking, and these ways of thinking eventually become automatic so that we may not be consciously aware of why we are seeing and understanding an event in a certain way.

The process of constructing our theory of the way of the world depends, according to Kelly, on seeing things as similar to or different from other things. Like a scientist, we test out our understanding of a new event against previous experience, asking ourselves, 'is this similar to or different from X?' Kelly also suggested that our world theory (or worldview) is hierarchical in that there are some elements of it which are core and are part of our identity, but these also include many subordinate elements, which in turn have their own subordinate elements, so that some areas (or constructs) of our unique theory of the world are more flexible and open to change than others.

Central to Kelly's theory is the individual and unique nature of our personal theories of the world. We make judgements about our own constructs of the world in relation to their usefulness. Kelly is clear to eschew any notion of a single or absolute truth. He is equally clear that to understand others, we need to try to understand how they are 'construing' the world, and so it follows that to understand ourselves better we need to understand how we are construing the world. Through this kind of understanding, we are able to develop, change and grow in self-awareness.

Whilst personal construct theory is not directly linked to theories of metacognition in the academic literature, both include this developmental reflective process; both are based on notions of constructivism; and both are concerned with individual subjectivity. It seemed apt then to use the methods associated with personal construct theory to engage teachers on the RE-flect project with thinking about how they construe the world. In particular, we wanted to focus on how teachers view RE, as this is likely to impact on how they teach RE. We could have used semi-structured interviews to ask teachers about their views and beliefs with regard to teaching RE, but we also wanted to facilitate the development of metacognition in terms of self-awareness. In addition, Kelly's theory suggests that many of the ways in which we construe the world whilst affecting our behaviour in the world are not conscious. So, we needed a method of bringing these understandings (or construals) of the world to consciousness so that they could be reflected upon and perhaps altered.

One of the main methods used in personal construct theory to elicit people's construals of the world is the repertory grid method. The next section describes the repertory grid (rep grid) method we used and gives some examples from one of the author's own rep grids.

The repertory grid method

Over the course of the project, teachers constructed at least two repertory grids. The first, at the start of the project, was on 'My Experience of RE'. This was aimed at teachers reflecting on how they had experienced RE as a child and as an adult. The second grid at the end of the project was titled 'Religious Education is ... '. This was aimed at teachers reflecting on what they think now about RE. Each grid was followed by a semi-structured interview and by the teachers' own reflective notes kept in their reflective diaries (see below).

In order to construct the grid, teachers were provided with a blank grid and eight small cards. Each card was to represent one element that the teacher considered important in relation to the topic of the grid, e.g. in the first grid, My Experience of RE, teachers discerned elements such as the name of the faith school they attended as a child; the name of the local vicar; philosophical writers they loved; events such as weddings, funerals or simply attending church; names of friends who had influenced them; particular religious practices; etc. Once the eight cards were complete, with one element on each card, these elements were written across the top of the grid. Then the process of discriminating could begin. In Kelly's theory we make meaning about the world from understanding how things compare to each other. The rep grid method involves selecting three of the eight cards at random and asking oneself how two are similar to each other but different from the third. It is important that this process is quick rather than involving a great deal of reflection. We are trying to tap into our unconscious, so the process is more akin to word association than deep contemplation. The similarity construct (C) is written on the left-hand side of the grid, and the difference construct (C) on the right-hand side. These form two poles: one representing similarity, the other representing difference. The cards are returned to the pack and re-shuffled so that a new combination of three cards is chosen. Cards will often appear in more than one selection, but the question is always how are two the same but different from the third. The process stops when the individual feels that they have no new construals. In our case, we limited the grid to ten constructs.

Once the constructs are in place, teachers were instructed to consider each element and decide whether it was more like the similarity pole, in which case it was given an X, or more like the difference pole, in which case it was given an O. Teachers worked through all of their elements, testing each against every similarity and difference pole to get a grid of Xs and Os. In order to discriminate further, we used a numerical rating from 1–5, so that if an element was construed as very like the similarity pole, it was given a rating of 1; if it was seen as very like the difference pole, it was given a rating of 5, and somewhere in the middle was given a rating of 3. Table 7.5 is an excerpt from one of the author's grids which we used as a model for how to construct grids. In this case, due to lack of space, the grid shows only four elements instead of the eight the teachers were encouraged to describe. Of course, each grid is wholly individual and unique. In Table 7.5, you can see that across the top are the elements I first wrote on my cards as elements of my own spirituality; these include: Listening to the Priest; Going on Retreat; and Reading Theology. I might also have added Flower Arranging or Visiting my Godmother. These elements are personal to me, and someone else asked to write elements for their own spirituality would come up with very different things. They could include more secular activities, such as Walking in Nature or Gardening. I shuffled my pack of cards and chose the top three cards. Then I asked in what ways were two of these elements similar to each other but different from the third? In this way, I created a construct with two poles. You can see in Table 7.5 that the first construct I came up with was Meditative/Intellectual. I returned the cards to the pack, shuffled again and chose the top three and asked the same question. This time I came up with the construct: Social Involvement/Individual. The degree to which the poles are opposites of each other is a personal interpretation. So, I may see meditative and intellectual as opposites, but someone else may not. The grid is entirely personal, and it is best at this early stage not to overthink the constructs. I continued in this way until I had ten constructs (Table 7.5 again shows only the first four of these). These constructs were written into the grid under the Similarity/Difference poles. At this stage, the constructs are no longer connected to any element.

Table 7.5 Exploration of my spirituality

Similarity Pole X Rated 1	E1 Listen to Priest	E2 Attend Mass	E3 Retreat	E4 Read Theology	Difference Pole 0 Rated 5
C1 Meditative	O4	X2	X1	O5	Intellectual
C2 Social Involvement	O4	X1	O4	O5	Individual
C3 Internal	X1	X2	X1	X2	External
C4 Challenging	X2	O5	X1	X2	Habitual

The choosing of three cards is used just to create constructs. Only then did I take the first element, Listening to the Priest, and asked myself if it was more like the similarity pole for construct 1 (Meditative) or more like the difference pole for construct 1 (Intellectual). You can see that I rated E1 (Listening to the Priest) as O4, i.e. as Intellectual, and quite strongly so, because I gave it a score of 4. In contrast, I rated E2 (Attending Mass) as more like the similarity pole for construct 1 (Meditative). I gave this a score of X2. So, whilst I saw it as more meditative than intellectual, the score of 2 showed that I did not see it as strongly meditative as E3 (Going on Retreat).

Once grids are constructed, it is possible to look for patterns and clusters and to reflect on why we might construe some things as similar and others as different. These processes are often formalised as 'laddering up and down', which allows for further elaboration of the framework. The process of laddering is a process of asking 'Why?' questions in laddering up, and 'What does it mean?' questions when laddering down. Teachers on the project were encouraged to engage in this laddering process for themselves, but it also formed part of the semi-structured interviews with researchers which followed the completion of each grid. The process of eliciting constructs and laddering up and down can bring up sensitive and emotional information. The process is both revelatory and thought-provoking. A common reaction is 'I never knew I thought about it like that', or 'now I understand why I see things in this way'. In drawing on teachers' personal and childhood experiences of RE, we were mindful of the possible emotionally sensitive material we were constructing.

The rep grid process does not suit everyone, and for one of our project teachers it was a difficult process. She commented,

> I understand entirely that how I present things is related to my own consciousness and that how I present things is going to affect how the children interpret them. But I found the rep grid process too personal for me, and it told me things about myself that I didn't know if I wanted to know. I don't think I really signed up for this.

This was not the case for everyone, however, and one teacher found the process better the second time she did it,

> I enjoyed the rep grid the second time, and I revisited the first one and that put a lot of questions in my head that I hadn't thought about and wanted to think about more. You can't do it in half an hour; it takes a lot of thought, but I found the more I did it, the more interested I became in the big questions that came up for me.

It is clear that the process needs to be used with caution and with some understanding that it can reveal difficult and painful things, but at the same time it can help us to understand our own view of the world and why we behave in particular ways in response to different situations. It brings back to consciousness ways of thinking and being which may have become automatic and habitual. We might also consider that if we ask pupils to reflect on themselves as thinkers and learners and to explore their responses to the world and its big questions, we might also, as teachers and educators, enter into the same process.

Reflective diaries

In addition to the repertory grids, teachers kept a reflective diary through the project. The diary was structured so that each month there was something different to reflect on and write about.

Teacher diary calendar

February

- Reflections on grid interview
- Laddering up and down

March

- How do my childhood experiences of RE relate to my beliefs now?
- Have my beliefs changed over time? – When and why?

April

- What do I think about Religious Education now?
- How does this relate to my own spirituality/faith/non-faith?

May

- What do I think about teaching RE? How confident do I feel? Why? What is my role as a teacher of RE?
- What kind of RE would I have liked as a child?

June

- Construct a new grid entitled, 'Religious Education is ... '
- Reflect on new grid – what does it tell me about myself in relation to RE?
- Ladder up and down some constructs and elements
- Compare this grid to the first one

July

- Reflect on this process of reflection. How has my thinking changed since the start of this project?

The purpose of both the constructing of rep grids and the reflective diary was to facilitate the development of teacher metacognition both in relation to themselves as a learner and thinker and in terms of how their own experiences and construals of the world affect their teaching of RE. It is clear from what teachers told us that they found the process revelatory and began to understand where their approach to RE teaching had come from and therefore how it might change; e.g. one teacher commented, 'So partly my own understanding of my own limitations make me want to give them [her pupils] a wider scope' and

> I've had to think about how much of, and what in my background is traditional, this is how it is, and what is my own philosophy now, and how has that come about, how is it that I'm convinced of some things now that I wasn't convinced of when I was 15, I can now go actually, no, I don't think so. How does that actually happen?

Questioning one's self in this way is metacognitive. The focus is on understanding one's own thinking and how that develops and changes over time. It was revealing that the interviews with teachers at the end of the project were more contemplative and included many more direct statements about their own thinking processes than the interviews we conducted at the beginning of the project. Through analysis of all the teacher data a number of themes stood out, including the following:

1. School attitude to RE at the start of the project
2. Childhood experiences of RE
3. Collective worship
4. Change in teaching
5. Child responses
6. Challenges

School attitude to RE at start of the project

A short survey of the participating teachers and others at the start of the project revealed that for many (but not all) schools, RE was quite a way down the agenda. Participating teachers' diaries revealed a feeling that school was often apathetic to RE, or in some cases deliberately in opposition to particular RE content. Supply staff, part-time or peripatetic staff were often tasked with teaching RE, and this led to a feeling of isolation and disempowerment. This was revealed in minor irritations related to the use of and ownership of classroom space, e.g. class teachers would take down RE displays without discussion with the RE teacher, or RE-designated space was used by the class teacher for literacy or artwork.

Childhood experiences of RE

Through the use of the rep grid technique, teachers reflected on their own childhood experiences of RE. These were varied, but one of the more common descriptions revolved around fear. This was seen in descriptions of adults involved in RE as seeming like angry giants. There were colourful descriptions of childhood experiences which had a myth-like quality, but which showed a good deal of anxiety around RE. For other participants, the most notable feeling was one of boredom. There were few instances of real enthusiasm for RE from childhood experiences.

Collective worship

There were many different forms of collective worship described, including virtual assemblies; attending church and secular assemblies, with variations and different configurations of these. Teachers spoke about opposition to faith-based assemblies both within some schools and from various external groups, including parents and school governors. Sometimes invited speakers were seen to conflict with the view of RE proposed in the RE-flect project, which created some difficulty for teachers trying to continue with the project against external pressure. Teachers reflected on the extent to which RE educators in their own past or in the present made their own values explicit with regard to different forms of collective worship. There was a feeling, too, that children often take part in collective worship with very little understanding of why they are taking part or what collective worship means.

Change in teaching

Through the reflective diaries and through reflecting on their own experiences of RE, teachers came to a clearer understanding of how they were construing RE, and this had an impact on the way they felt RE should be taught. Thus, teachers talked about how they had given children more freedom in RE lessons but found them to be more motivated towards RE. Some of the teachers had changed the focus away from literacy and an end product (be it a drawing or a piece of writing) to focus on children understanding and being able to talk about issues of faith and no faith. Teachers also spoke of slowing down the RE lessons to give children more of a chance to reflect on their own position in relation to others and to be able to articulate their thinking. There was a sense from the childhood experiences that most teachers did not want to replicate the type of RE they had experienced themselves but also a feeling that in trying not to do that they had perhaps lost the RE focus altogether in some cases.

Child responses

Teachers reflected on changes in their RE classes during the project. In particular, there was notable change in the way children reacted to RE. Thus, teachers spoke of an increase in meaningful questions from children; rather than simple questions about how to do a task or asking for task clarification, children began to ask deeper questions about different religious faiths and about faith in general. Teachers reported on better group discussion skills and a general increase in tolerance between pupils more generally. In contrast to some of the teachers' own experiences of RE, they found that children in the RE-flect classes were showing more enthusiasm and motivation for RE.

Challenges

Many of the challenges teachers expressed are common to most research-led intervention programmes. These include the problem of maintaining the project work after the project has ended, particularly when only one teacher in a school has taken part. The reflective diaries and rep grids showed that teachers had changed their view of RE teaching, and this seemed to translate into some more permanent change in future practice regardless of external and contextual factors. A further challenge relevant to this particular project was the sensitive nature of the content of RE, and teachers, although still grappling with this issue, felt a renewed sense of confidence to be able to deal with specific topics. This also included working with and including parents in the wider discussion around RE.

Conclusion

Through a process of reflection, including keeping reflective diaries and constructing a rep grid, project teachers became more aware of how their unconscious states were affecting their behaviour both inside and outside of the classroom. Revealing past experiences was often an emotional experience, but those who did it found it had a lasting effect on their teaching practice and also on their self-awareness. Understanding how our unconscious construals of the world affect our behaviour gives us more power to change the way we think and behave. Similarly, enabling children to discuss difficult and profound issues of faith, belief and spirituality encourages tolerance for other belief systems, self-awareness and self-regulated learning.

Further reading

Jankowicz, D. (2004) *The Easy Guide to Repertory Grids*. Chichester, UK: John Wiley and Sons Ltd.

Kelly, G.A. (1977) 'Personal construct theory and the psychotherapeutic interview'. *Cognitive Therapy and Research*, 1 (4), 355–362.

Larkin, S. (2015) 'Metacognitive learning environments: An approach to metacognition research'. In R. Wegerif, L. Li and J.C. Kaufman (eds.), *The Routledge International Handbook of Research on Teaching Thinking*. Oxford, UK: Routledge, 254–265.

Conclusion 8

This chapter provides a summary of the key elements of the RE-flect approach with reference to the three metacognitive learning environment zones and the Lesson Planning Framework. The chapter summarises the strengths and challenges of the approach and how it might be implemented in any RE classroom. It also explains how the principles might be adapted for use in other phases of education and/or applied across the curriculum. The chapter concludes with some further recommendations for teaching and learning in RE, building on the experiences and findings of the RE-flect project, as well as positing a vision of how the foci of the three metacognitive learning environment zones can be balanced and integrated.

A socio-cultural metacognitive environment

Metacognition describes the reflective nature of the human mind. Approaches to learning that promote metacognition aim to help learners think explicitly about the cognitive processes involved in learning. This includes teaching them to take responsibility for their own learning, to set learning goals and to monitor, regulate and evaluate their learning dispositions, processes and progress. Research from across the curriculum, including English, Mathematics and Science, suggests that such approaches have high levels of positive impact upon pupils' academic achievement, especially when undertaken in mutually supportive collaborative groups. Witnessing that RE was lagging behind other curriculum areas in recognising the benefits of metacognition, the RE-flect project sought to explore the potential of such approaches within RE and specifically in relation to socio-cultural metacognitive approaches.

A socio-cultural approach to fostering metacognition requires a change in classroom cultures and impacts upon every aspect of the learning environment, including changes in the motivation, attitudes and metacognitive abilities of teachers and pupils. The aim is to create a safe psycho-social space in which pupils are supported and empowered to learn together; to develop their own individual self-awareness and self-concept as learners; and in which every teacher–pupil and pupil–pupil interaction promotes learning dispositions, enhances cognitive and metacognitive abilities and challenges emotive blocks to learning. The bedrock to such an approach is the relationships established between teachers and pupils which need, amongst other things, to be genuine, authentic, collaborative, empowering and recurrently evidencing the ability to role model metacognitive abilities.

On the RE-flect project, to promote the conditions conducive to a metacognitive orientation, we asked teachers to create three physical zones within their classrooms: (1) a meta-thinking zone (promoting thinking about thinking and learning in RE); (2) a worldview zone (promoting thinking about oneself as a learner in RE); and (3) a resources zone (promoting thinking about representations of (non-)religious phenomena in RE). We hoped that teachers and pupils would feel a sense of ownership of, belonging to and community in this environment. We also hoped that it would allow for periods of reflection and quiet, whilst being flexible enough to facilitate different tasks and activities.

Meta-thinking zone

The meta-thinking zone was envisaged to facilitate a shift in thinking from the cognitive to the metacognitive level. As there is reciprocity between the development of a language of thinking and the development of metacognitive knowledge, a key aim was to develop in teachers and pupils a vocabulary by which to talk about thinking. This included mental state words, such as believe, know, understand, think, imagine, guess and remember. We wanted the inner voices of teachers and pupils to speak aloud, acting as a model for others and encouraging the development of everybody's individual metacognitive voice.

The meta-thinking zone was also designed to develop three different aspects of metacognition. The first was metacognitive knowledge, which pertains to awareness of the cognitive processes by which we obtain knowledge and the conditions relating to these processes. For this, pupils need to develop (1) knowledge of themselves, specifically in relation to their thinking processes (e.g. self-knowledge and self-evaluation); (2) knowledge of the task at hand (e.g. the aims and methods of RE generally, and the specific objectives and parameters of each learning activity and process); and (3) knowledge of the strategies they employ to learn and evaluate their learning (e.g. the means to the end and its efficacy). The principal means of engendering metacognitive knowledge is through teacher–pupil, pupil–pupil and pupil–self questioning, and by inviting pupils to make conscious, and perhaps verbalise, their thoughts or feelings about the tasks with which they are faced. This can be achieved by creating complex, open-ended tasks that require planning, collaboration and decision-making, as well as metacognitive reflection and communication. Thereby, further developing their self-concept and reflective self-awareness, pupils can be encouraged to reflect on their knowledge, abilities and experiences as learners in general, and how they approach thinking and learning in RE specifically. This can be achieved by being attentive and committed to answering such questions as 'What is there to be known?', 'What do I know already?', 'How do I know that?', 'What more do I need to know?' and 'How can I learn that?'

The second aspect of metacognition to be developed by the meta-thinking zone was monitoring and control. This refers to the often subconscious self-regulatory processes by which we track our thinking, correct errors, stop and reflect and change course. These processes can be made conscious if individuals and groups are taught explicit strategies by which to plan, monitor and evaluate their learning, and then are given opportunities to implement them, both with and without support. This involves teaching pupils (1) planning, in terms of adopting general strategies and specific techniques to learning, including knowing when planning is helpful; (2) monitoring, in terms of identifying turning points and staging posts in the learning process; and (3) evaluating, in terms of deploying success criteria and learning lessons for the future.

The third aspect of metacognition to be developed by the meta-thinking zone was metacognitive experiences. This refers to the ability of self-regulating learners to become aware of, and to manage, their emotional responses to a learning situation (e.g. feeling confident or unconfident, finding something easy or difficult or being interested or bored). These experiences might be brief or lengthy, simple or complex. Teachers can promote the ability to recognise and manage these metacognitive experiences at the level of the individual or the group, reminding pupils that it is valid and important to reflect on their feelings as learners and that their feelings about a task may stay the same or change.

Through each of the above aspects of metacognition, pupils would reflect on their thinking and learning and learn how to think and learn in RE. By developing greater awareness of themselves as learners and by abstracting general principles of learning, pupils are better able to transfer the knowledge, understanding and skills they construct during one activity and situation, not only to problems which are similar in content or structure (near transfer), but also to problems which may be more complex and open-ended than the original task (far transfer). This has implications for cross-curricular learning and lifelong learning.

Worldview zone

The worldview zone was designed to enable pupils to become aware of their own personal worldviews (i.e. their personal identities, ultimate/existential beliefs, ontologies and epistemologies, values and ethical principles). Worldviews are integral to educational experiences, both influencing and being influenced by learning processes and affecting learners' dispositions, motivations and emotions. Worldview consciousness enables pupils to understand their own interpretation of, and engagement with, curriculum content, and to engage more deeply and in more genuine dialogue with the opinions of others. In both cases, the 'subject matter' might conform to or contradict the pupils' personal perspectives, thereby potentially creating a perplexing learning environment in which their frames of reference, habits of mind and points of view are challenged or changed. By making each learner's subjectivity an object of study, it can be shown how self-efficacy judgements can affect learning outcomes and how worldviews can influence pupils' interest and enjoyment of what they are learning about and their perceptions of its significance and relevance.

To promote pupils' knowledge, or metacognitive knowledge, about their own developing worldviews, pupils are provided with opportunities to engage in personal evaluation, self-reflection and reflexivity. On the RE-flect project, in a systematic, in-depth, continuous and methodical manner, pupils were required to capture in Worldview Profiles (a form of reflective diary) their responses to questions contained within a Worldview Question Framework. It represented a practical method by which pupils were encouraged (1) to recognise, reflect upon, understand and articulate their own worldviews; (2) to compare and contrast their personal worldviews with those of others; and (3) to explain how their worldviews influence, or are influenced by, their learning about religion(s) and other worldview(s). The purpose was to enable pupils, as far as possible, to monitor and regulate their subjectivity as learners and to teach them how positioning and partiality can influence the nature and purpose of learning, meaning-making and knowledge-producing processes.

Resources zone

The final space in our metacognitive learning environment was the resources zone to which teachers and pupils could bring items, artefacts, books and other resources relevant to the topic being studied. It sought to encourage pupils to develop respect both for the physical objects and what they represented. Multiple resources representing single topics, or single resources representing multiple topics, provide pupils with an opportunity to engage with a plurality of perspectives, meanings and interpretations. The 'objects' support pupils' exploration of the issue of representation; for example, the nature and purpose of signs and symbols, the differences between religious phenomena and resources chosen to embody or signify them and the criteria by which resources are chosen and arranged (as opposed to rejected and omitted). Through the process of engagement, relationships and connections could be established between resources, between pupils and between the resources and pupils.

It was thought that the process of constructing the resources zone would create a sense of ownership, togetherness and community, which is a key component of a metacognitive learning environment. Moreover, participation in the 'crowdsourcing' of content and resources has the potential to enable teachers and pupils to see that the curriculum is socially constructed, contingent and provisional and, as a consequence, no knowledge about religion(s) and worldview(s), and religious and non-religious phenomena, is unproblematic and incontestable. Through raising the questions, 'What are the objects of study?', 'How do we gain knowledge and understanding of them?' and 'What relevance, meaning and significance do they have for us?', pupils would be encouraged to think about researching and representing religion(s) and worldview(s); the evidence, sources and data required for doing so; and how and why knowledge content is selected and sequenced.

From theory to lesson planning

To aid the implementation of the previously mentioned pedagogical principles, the teachers participating in the RE-flect project were provided with a Lesson Planning Framework and general guidance on how to implement a metacognitive approach. In summary, when synthesised, these called for:

- A clear aim or focus (e.g. lesson objective or learning outcome);
- Sustained attentiveness to pupils' prior learning and existing knowledge, and what they need to find out and learn;
- Promoting pupil reflection on, and reflective dialogue about, their own worldviews, thinking and learning and the relationships between these elements;
- Developing a language of thinking, including metaphors and images of learning;
- Providing opportunities for pupils to take responsibility for, and to explain, their thinking and learning, and their planning, monitoring and evaluating strategies;
- Collaborative learning opportunities, social interaction and active exchanging of ideas;
- Encouraging pupils to engage with material/resources in each of the three metacognitive learning zones;
- Understanding pupil perceptions of relevance and significance;
- Planned opportunities to gather evidence of pupils' metacognitive abilities; and
- Opportunities for pupils to evaluate their learning, including the knowledge, understanding and skills that were (not) acquired; the effectiveness of the strategies; and the relationship between worldviews, learning processes and subject matter.

An approach such as this places equal emphasis on process and product, knowledge and skills and the learner, learning and learned. There is nothing to preclude it from being adapted for use in RE in secondary schools, Religious Studies in further education colleges or even Theology and Religious Studies in higher education. Furthermore, other than the subject matter, the approach is not peculiar to the study of religion(s) and worldview(s). In any curriculum subject, perhaps most especially other humanities and social science subjects, pupils can be expected to develop metacognitive knowledge of self, tasks and strategies; exercise self-regulatory abilities through planning, monitoring and evaluating; manage metacognitive experiences; engage in personal evaluation and self-reflection; and undertake the process of gathering and analysing evidence, sources and data. Indeed, it is hoped that pupils will be able to transfer learning across subject domains so that understanding self, others, tasks and goals become common cross-curricular practices. Subject specificity comes about as a result of an orientation towards selected objects of study; the recognition that positionality and subjectivity play out in distinctive ways according to subject matter; the setting of certain kinds of task with associated parameters; and the utilisation of a particular range of strategies. Here, school curriculum subjects represent traditions of practice that are the outcomes of complex change and continuity over time in response to multiple factors, including political traditions, religious sectarianism, competing ideologies and vested interests relating to status, power and resources. During the RE-flect project we were constantly reminded of this.

From planning to implementation

As has been made clear throughout this book, the journey from rhetoric to reality, from theory to practice and from the prescribed to the enacted is a long and winding road when it comes to pedagogical and curricular innovation. It involves a plethora of potential wrong turns, leading to dead ends or undesirable destinations, as well as roundabouts by which one might end up returning home. If we began the RE-flect project with the assumption that existing pedagogical and curricular traditions could be transformed by conviction, good management, planning and resources, then we ended feeling slightly overwhelmed by systemic barriers to change and local impediments to effective practice. The national picture relating to RE is one of under-resourcing at almost every level of operation, and of the multiple stakeholders repeatedly attempting to marginalise or centralise; abolish or reform; or develop or envelop the subject. The challenges currently facing the subject have been laid out previously, but a few are worth repeating again because of their impact upon our research: the paucity of suitably qualified and specialist teachers of RE; the deficiency of relevant initial and continuing professional development provision; and the ongoing and seemingly irresolvable debates about the nature, aims and purposes of RE. These challenges are important to bear in mind in terms of contextualising the least successful elements of the RE-flect project.

Outcomes in context

The ability and confidence of participant teachers to turn our pedagogical and curricular theories into classroom practices were affected by: not being the main class teacher; not having obtained a relevant subject-specialist teaching qualification; and/or not possessing the most relevant academic disciplinary background (e.g. Theology or Religious Studies). Initial appraisals of the quality of RE being undertaken at the start of the project revealed, at worst, relatively superficial engagement with religion(s) and worldview(s), a lack of awareness of the local Agreed Syllabus (where relevant) and both teacher and pupil confusion regarding the nature and purpose of RE and the means by which it should be taught and assessed. When RE is taught by somebody substituting the main class teacher, it is inevitably hampered by the quality of the teacher–pupil relationships. In a metacognitive approach, critical moments in the learning of individuals and groups need to be recognised and the learning potential of metacognitive knowledge, processes and experiences needs to be exploited. It is hard to be attentive and attuned to the inner voice of pupils, and to intervene appropriately in their tasks and activities, if you are not already familiar with their actual voices. As a consequence of these background factors, a project that sought to enable teachers to refine and enhance their existing learning environments had to begin by providing some basic maps of the terrain and some simple navigational tools.

By the end of the project, however, teachers recounted that their perceptions of, and practices in, RE were very different. Having engaged in developmental reflective processes, they had grown in self-awareness, in terms of how they were construing the world, religion(s) and worldview(s) and most importantly, RE. Even whilst recognising feelings of fear, anxiety, isolation and disempowerment as RE teachers, they became more enthusiastic and confident about the subject as the project progressed and developed a more sophisticated understanding of its nature and purpose. This had an impact on their teaching. The pace of lessons slowed, and the depth of pupil engagement increased. For some, a previous emphasis on literacy and delivering an end product gave way to a focus upon the processes of understanding and reflecting upon matters of faith and no faith.

According to the teachers, the pupils became more active learners, leading discussions, asking and answering deeper questions and making connections between subject content. They also appeared to be more motivated, both enjoying the subject more and learning more. The greater clarity by which pupils talked about RE mirrored the improvement in their attainment. There was lots of evidence of pupils shifting their thinking from their own perspective to see and understand the perspective of others, both in terms of the curriculum content and in their collaborative working with other pupils. In this regard, they appeared more tolerant and respectful. There were also occasions on which pupils confidently expressed puzzlement, frustration, disappointment and sometimes hostility towards the task, thereby evidencing an ability to recognise and manage metacognitive experiences.

With regard to the use of Worldview Profiles, the pupils generally commented favourably, despite the wide diversity of practices between the schools. In particular, they praised the provision of a confidential space in which to write personal reflections. Some of the entries were careful, reflective and addressing questions they had not previously considered. The very best, evidencing conceptual understanding and utilising appropriate vocabulary, had clearly been written following relevant teacher input and whole class or small group discussions. The teachers' evaluations of the approach, and the extent to which it achieved its aims, were also almost wholly positive. They believed worldview profiling was stimulating and engaging, offering pupils the opportunity to communicate and justify their own ideas and to discuss and give reasons for their beliefs and values. For them, it had clear educational benefits.

Yet the Worldview Profiles also laid bare the extent to which the participant teachers needed further permission, encouragement and support with regard to designing and implementing activities that were both faithful to the theoretical underpinnings of the project and could spark pupils' interest in, and scaffold their thinking about, their developing worldviews. Ideally, pupils should have been engaged in reflection on their worldviews before, during and after learning episodes in RE to increase the chances of deep, meaningful and critical engagement with (non-)religious subject matter. However, at times formulaic written entries of pupils made little reference to subject content knowledge or the processes involved in learning about religion(s) and worldview(s). There was room for further development of pupils reflecting on how their worldviews influence and are influenced by their learning or how they compare and contrast with the worldviews of others. Even if the Worldview Profiles were rich in terms of metacognitive knowledge, they were sometimes poor in terms of RE subject-content knowledge. The purpose of worldview profiling was to improve the capacity of pupils to learn about religion(s) and worldview(s) and to improve the quality of that learning. It was not an end in itself, and we never set out to create imbalanced RE that was metacognitively heavy but light in terms of engagement with (non-)religious institutional worldviews. Overall, it was clear that additional thought needs to be given to the integration of worldview profiling within RE, and this relates to fundamental questions about the subject's nature and purpose.

An academic and scholarly context for (meta)cognition

One of the original assumptions of the RE-flect project team was that the creation of a socio-cultural metacognitive learning environment in RE will contribute positively to the fulfilment of the subject's aims and objectives regardless of what these are. This is because it draws upon well-founded and long-standing generic pedagogical and psychological knowledge rather than subject-specific pedagogical and curricular theories and concepts that are rooted in particular movements, discourses, models, paradigms, etc. Its validity is not contingent upon any particular resolution to fundamental debates about the definition or meaning of religion(s) and worldview(s) or the most fruitful way of studying religion(s) and worldview(s). In theory, all forms of RE, regardless of the research methodologies or teaching pedagogies upon which they are based, could be enhanced by a metacognitive approach. Thus, there could be many metacognitive forms of RE, each enhancing teaching and learning with regard to different subject aims, methods and contents. However, this insight does little to help the non-specialist practitioner, committed to improving standards but confused about the nature and purpose of the subject and about what knowledge, skills and values are required of both teachers and pupils alike. For this reason, at this point, we would like to outline a more holistic vision.

In the context of state-maintained schools without a religious affiliation, we believe the ability of teachers to plan, teach and assess would be heightened by couching the aims and purposes of inclusive multi-faith RE predominantly in academic and scholarly terms that cohere with the long-standing, subject-based, cognitively orientated and assessment-driven core curriculum of most schools. For the majority of the last 150 years of state-maintained schooling, pupils have been expected to demonstrate the attainment of core knowledge and skills in order to show progress and, when necessary, pass examinations in a range of discrete curriculum subjects, e.g. Mathematics and English. RE has not always aligned itself to this model. At different times and in different places, its aspirations have related more to the devotional, practical and pastoral, for example. In our view, a narrower, and more focused vision, is required. In RE, pupils should be learning about religion(s) and worldview(s) and learning about the study of religion(s) and worldview(s). Furthermore, we believe the distinguishing aims, contents and methods of RE should be aligned to the most pertinent disciplines in higher education from which the knowledge-base of RE should be derived. This is not an uncontroversial vision, particularly from the perspectives of those who define RE primarily in terms of its contribution to the spiritual, moral, social and cultural development of pupils, and/or those for whom 'Religious Education' is so named because it describes the religious nature and purpose of the educational process.

The subjectivity, partiality and positioning of pupils is a powerful determinant of how they approach the study of religion(s) and worldview(s), and in absolute terms, they will emerge transformed and developed by their learning experiences, perhaps particularly when metacognitive self-knowledge, personal evaluation and self-reflection are promoted. However, in schools without a religious affiliation, it would be inappropriate to predetermine the nature of the transformation or deliberately plan for the direction of development. For this reason, we do not think spiritual, moral, social and cultural development can serve as a legitimate justification for, or primary purpose of, RE in such schools. The past, present and probable future significance of religion(s) and worldview(s) provides sufficient justification for mandating their study in schools without a religious affiliation. As a discrete and specialist subject devoted to this end, we believe the purpose of inclusive multi-faith RE should be to provide pupils with the knowledge, skills, attributes and values associated with the communities of academic inquiry concerned with the study of religion(s) and worldview(s), for example, through theological, religious and related studies. This includes understanding the connection between (1) who they are as pupils, what they believe and value, how they live their lives and so on; and (2) their capacity and motivation as learners to develop knowledge and understanding of other people's identities, worldviews, practices and so forth. This critical reflexivity is justified in terms of academic and scholarly learning processes and outcomes, rather than faith formation, religious nurture or spiritual development.

A metacognitive approach would provide pupils, at an appropriate conceptual level, with the language, knowledge, skills and experiences by which they can begin tackling, from the most rudimentary starting points, issues that go right to the heart of any academic or scholarly study of religion(s) and worldview(s). This includes raising profound questions about personal identity (the worldview, characteristics, knowledge and skills of the learner), ontology (the nature of [non-]religious objects of study), epistemology (the nature of truth, belief, knowledge and understanding) and methodology (the intellectual and practical strategies to be deployed in the inquiry process). In simpler terms, it involves reflection on what is being learnt about religion(s) and worldview(s); reflection on how to learn about religion(s) and worldview(s); and reflection on oneself as a learner learning about religion(s) and worldview(s). To do justice to each of these elements, a balance must be established between the three foci of our metacognitive zones (see Table 8.1).

At the same time as creating a balance between these dimensions, it is also important to establish the connections between them. This was particularly lacking in the utilisation of Worldview Profiles by teachers and pupils. Designing lessons or units of work as shared inquiries is one method of explicitly and coherently manifesting all of the hallmarks of our socio-cultural metacognitive approach (as summarised in the Lesson Planning Framework). In retrospect, after the completion of the project, it is clear we should have advocated this

Table 8.1 The three learning dimensions in the RE-flect approach

Resources Zone	curriculum content and issues of representation	what is being learnt about and why	knowledge and understanding of religion(s) and RE
Meta-Thinking Zone	tasks, strategies and learning processes	how it is being learnt about and why	knowledge of and ability to apply skills used in the study of religion(s)
Worldview Zone	personal evaluation and self-reflection	who is the learner, and why this matters	knowledge of worldviews and how they influence and are influenced by learning about religion(s)

to teachers more strongly. A shared inquiry might begin with a problem or issue relating to a given religious/worldview topic. Pupil curiosity can be stimulated through exposure to existing knowledge in the form of their own and other people's representations of religion(s) and worldview(s) (e.g. teacher, textbook writer, website developer and television documentary scriptwriter), as well as by reflection on their own worldviews and how they might influence, or be influenced by, learning about the subject matter. Second, a salient question can be identified to focus the exploration of the topic, and activities and strategies can be planned collaboratively by the teacher and/or pupils. Third, the inquiry strategies can be implemented and monitored by individuals and/or groups, so as to facilitate the necessary learning about religion(s) and worldview(s). The objects and resources by which religions and worldviews are represented in the classroom can be analysed and discussed, providing pupils with an opportunity to make sense of and make meaning from them. Throughout the inquiry process, pupils can be encouraged to reflect on how they are learning, the challenges they face and the ways in which they might improve their learning. Finally, as part of the process of concluding the inquiry, pupils can be given an opportunity to evaluate the extent to which the inquiry achieved its objectives; the strengths and weaknesses of the learning process; how far (if at all) their initial thinking had been challenged and extended; and the questions, problems and issues that remain or have now arisen.

Conceived in this way, it is not difficult to see the link between RE as a metacognitively enriched, inquiry-led curriculum subject in schools, and theological, religious and related studies as multi-disciplinary research fields in higher education institutions. Both are involved in constructing, de-constructing and re-constructing knowledge about religion(s), worldview(s) and cognate subject matter. Parallels can be drawn both between researching and learning, and between the methodological and pedagogical. The studies of both school pupils and academic researchers are enhanced when critical reflexivity is demonstrated about the fundamental assumptions underpinning and influencing their scholarship. Metacognitive dialogues about selves, tasks and strategies mirror research debates about (inter-)subjectivity, hermeneutics, methodologies and methods.

On this basis, we can conclude by reiterating our recommendation that the purpose of inclusive multi-faith RE in schools without a religious affiliation should be to provide pupils with the knowledge, skills, attributes and values associated with the communities of academic inquiry concerned with the study of religion(s) and worldview(s), for example, through theological, religious and related studies. To this end, a socio-cultural, metacognitively enriched and inquiry-led approach would seek to (1) initiate pupils into hermeneutically and methodologically orientated dialogues (including debates about the nature of religion(s) and worldview(s) and how knowledge about religion(s) and worldview(s) is created); (2) offer pupils personal experience of learning about religion(s) and worldview(s), reflecting upon their own knowledge, abilities and experiences as learners; (3) stimulate pupil reflection on their own and other people's positionality, and how personal worldviews affect, and are affected by, learning processes; and (4) enable pupils independently and collaboratively to plan, monitor and evaluate inquiries, drawing upon strategies deployed by scholars of religion(s) and worldview(s). Thereby, the foci of the three metacognitive learning environment zones deployed in the RE-flect project could be balanced and integrated through shared inquiries that are focused on clear aims, objectives and outcomes, and undertaken by pupils aware of their own cognitive processes and learning strategies. This ambition can be realised, but only if teachers and pupils have the willingness and ability to make it so. Above all else, in the development of this inclination and aptitude, they will need time to reflect.

Bibliography

All Party Parliamentary Group for Religious Education. (2013) *RE: The truth unmasked: The supply of and support for religious education teachers*. Online. http://religiouseducationcouncil.org.uk/appg/news/2013-03-18/appg-re-final-report-the-truth-unmasked (accessed 7 June 2018).

Ambridge, B. (2015) *10 myths about psychology: Debunked*. Online. www.youtube.com/watch?v=ce31WjiVcY0 (accessed 7 June 2018).

Anderson, L.W. and Krathwohl, D.R. (2000) *A Taxonomy for Learning, Teaching and Assessing*. Essex, UK: Pearson.

Ardila, A. (2008) 'On the evolutionary origins of executive functions'. *Brain and Cognition*, 68 (1), 92–99.

Baker, L. (1994) 'Fostering metacognitive development'. In: H.W. Reese (ed.), *Advances in Child Development and Behaviour* (Vol. 25). San Diego, CA: Academic Press, 201–239.

Baumfield, V. (2010) 'Towards a pedagogy for Religious Education: Professional development through engagement in and with research'. *British Journal of Religious Education*, 32 (2), 89–91.

Blaylock, L. (2000) 'Issues in achievement and assessment in religious education in England: Which way should we turn?' *British Journal of Religious Education*, 23 (1), 45–58.

Blaylock, L., Gent, B., Stern, J. and Walshe, K. (2013) *Subject Review of Religious Education in England, Phase 1: Report of the Expert Panel*. London: Religious Education Council of England and Wales.

Bloom, B. (1956) *Taxonomy of Educational Objectives: The Classification of Educational Goals*. London: Longmans.

Carpendale, J.I. and Chandler, M.J. (1996) 'On the distinction between false belief understanding and subscribing to an interpretive theory of mind'. *Child Development*, 67 (4), 1686–1706.

Cary, M. and Reder, L. (2002) 'Metacognition in strategy selection: Giving consciousness too much credit'. In: P. Chambers, M. Izaute and P.-J. Marescaux (eds.) *Metacognition: Process, Function and Use*. Dordrecht, the Netherlands: Kluwer Academic Publishers, 63–77.

Chandler, D. (1995) *The Act of Writing: A Media Theory Approach*. Aberystwyth, UK: Prifysgol Cymru.

Chater, M. and Erricker, C. (2013) *Does Religious Education Have a Future: Pedagogical and Policy Prospects*. Abingdon, UK: Routledge.

Clarke, C. and Woodhead, L. (2015) *A New Settlement: Religion and Beliefs in Schools*. Lancaster, UK: Westminster Faith Debates.

Coffield, F., Moseley, D., Hall, E. and Ecclestone, K. (2004) *Learning Styles and Pedagogy in Post-16 Learning: A Systematic and Critical Review*. London: Learning and Skills Research Centre.

Commission on Religious Education. (2018) *Final Report: Religion and Worldviews: The Way Forward*. London: Religious Education Council of England and Wales.

Conroy, J., Lundie, D., Davis, R.A., Baumfield, V., Barnes, L.P., Gallagher, T., Lowden, K., Bourque, N. and Wenell, K. (2013) *Does Religious Education Work? A Multidimensional Investigation*. London: Bloomsbury Press.

Copley, T. and Priestley, J. (1991) *Forms of Assessment in Religious Education. The Main Report of the FARE Project*. Exeter, UK: FARE Project.

Crooks, S. and Soucy, A. (2015) 'Course design in religious studies: An experiment in metacognitive education'. *Studies in Religion*, 44 (1), 91–105.

Department for Children, Schools and Families. (2010) *Religious Education in English Schools: Non-Statutory Guidance 2010*. Nottingham, UK: Department for Children, Schools and Families.

Department for Education. (2014) National curriculum and assessment from September 2014: information for schools. Online. www.gov.uk/government/ uploads/system/uploads/attachmentdata/file/358070/ NCassessmentquals factsheetSeptupdate.pdf. (accessed 17 June 2018).

Devon County Council. (2005) *How Well Am I Doing in RE? Assessment in Religious Education*. Exeter, UK: Devon County Council.

Diana, R.A. and Reder, L.M. (2004) 'Visual versus verbal metacognition: Are they really different?' In: D.T. Levin (ed.), *Thinking and Seeing: Visual Metacognition in Adults and Children*. Cambridge, MA: MIT/Bradford Books, 187–202.

Dinham, A. and Shaw, M. (2015) *RE for REal: The Future of Teaching and Learning about Religion and Belief*. London: Goldsmiths', University of London.

Dunlosky, J., Bottiroli, S. and Hartwig, M. (2009) 'Sins committed in the name of ecological validity: A call for representative design in education science'. In: D.J. Hacker, J. Dunlosky and A.C. Graesser (eds.), *Handbook of Metacognition in Education*. New York: Routledge, 430–440.

Efklides, A. (2002) 'The systemic nature of metacognitive experiences'. In: P. Chambers, M. Izaute and P.-J. Marescaux (eds.), *Metacognition: Process, Function and Use*. Dordrecht, the Netherlands: Kluwer Academic Publishers, 19–34.

Elliott, A. (1993) 'Metacognitive teaching strategies and young children's mathematical learning'. Paper presented at the Annual Conference of the Australian Association for Research in Education (AARE), Fremantle, Australia, November.

Erricker, C., Sullivan, D., Ota, C., Erricker, J. and Logan, J. (1994) 'The development of children's world views'. *Journal of Beliefs & Values*, 15 (2), 3–6.

Fancourt, N. (2005) 'Challenges for self-assessment in religious education'. *British Journal of Religious Education*, 27 (2), 115–125.

Fancourt, N. (2010) '"I'm less intolerant": Reflexive self-assessment in religious education'. *British Journal of Beliefs & Values*, 35 (3), 291–305.

Fancourt, N. (2014) 'Re-defining "learning about religion" and "learning from religion"'. *British Journal of Religious Education*, 37 (2), 122–137.

Flavell, J.H. (1979) 'Metacognition and cognitive monitoring: A new area of cognitive-developmental inquiry'. *American Psychologist*, 34 (10), 906–911.

Flavell, J.H. (2000) 'Developing intuitions about the mental experiences of self and others'. Paper presented at the Meeting of the Jean Piaget Society, Montreal, Canada, June.

Fraser, B.J. (1998) 'Classroom environment instruments: Development, validity and applications'. *Learning Environments Research*, 1 (1), 7–34.

Freathy, G., Freathy, R., Doney, J., Walshe, K. and Teece, G. (2015) *The RE-Searchers: A New Approach to Primary Religious Education*. Exeter, UK: University of Exeter.

Graesser, A.C. and Person, N.K. (1994) 'Question asking during tutoring'. *American Educational Research Journal*, 31 (1), 104–137.

Greenfield, S. (2000) *Brain Story*. London: BBC Worldwide.

Grimmitt, M. (1987) *Religious Education and Human Development: The Relationship between Studying Religions and Personal, Social and Moral Education*. Great Wakering, UK: McCrimmons.

Hatano, G. and Inagaki, K. (1992) 'Desituating cognition through the construction of conceptual knowledge'. In: P. Light and G. Butterworth (eds.), *Context and Cognition: Ways of Learning and Knowing*. Hillsdale, NJ: Lawrence Erlbaum, 115–133.

Homan, R. (2000) 'Don't let the murti get dirty: The uses and abuses of religious "artefacts"'. *British Journal of Religious Education*, 23 (1), 27–37.
Jackson, R. (1997) *Religious Education: An Interpretive Approach*. London: Hodder and Stoughton.
Jankowicz, D. (2004) *The Easy Guide to Repertory Grids*. Chichester, UK: John Wiley and Sons.
Johnston, W. (1983) *The Mirror Mind: Spirituality and Transformation*. London: William Collins.
Juliebö, M., Malicky, G. and Norman, C. (1998) 'Metacognition of young readers in an early intervention programme'. *Journal of Research in Reading*, 21 (1), 24–35.
Jurado, M.B. and Rosselli, M. (2007) 'The elusive nature of executive functions: A review of our current understanding'. *Neuropsychology Review*, 17 (3), 213–233.
Kelly, G.A. (1955/1991) *The Psychology of Personal Constructs*. Volumes 1 and 2. First published by Norton, 1955, then by Routledge in collaboration with the Centre for Personal Construct Psychology, 1991.
Kelly, G.A. (1977) 'Personal construct theory and the psychotherapeutic interview'. *Cognitive Therapy and Research*, 1 (4), 355–362.
Langer, E. (1997) *The Power of Mindful Learning*. Reading, MA: Addison-Wesley.
Larkin, S. (2010) *Metacognition in Young Children*. Oxford, UK: Routledge.
Larkin, S. (2015) 'Metacognitive learning environments: An approach to metacognition research'. In: R. Wegerif, L. Li and J.C. Kaufman (eds.), *The Routledge International Handbook of Research on Teaching Thinking*. Oxford, UK: Routledge, 254–265.
Larkin, S., Freathy, R., Walshe, K. and Doney, J. (2014) 'Creating metacognitive environments in primary school RE classrooms'. *Journal of Beliefs & Values*, 35 (2), 175–186.
Leopold, C. and Leutner, D. (2015) 'Improving students' science text comprehension through metacognitive self-regulation when applying learning strategies'. *Metacognition and Learning*, 10 (3), 313–346.
Lilienfeld, S.O., Lynn, S.J., Ruscio, J. and Beyerstein, B.L. (2010) *50 Great Myths of Popular Psychology: Shattering Widespread Misconceptions about Human Behavior*. Chichester, UK: Wiley-Blackwell.
Lilly, J., Peacock, A., Shoveller, S. and Struthers, D. (2014) *Beyond Levels: Alternative Assessment Approaches Developed by Teaching Schools*. Nottingham, UK: National College for Teaching and Leadership.
Lockl, K. and Schneider, W. (2006) 'Precursors of metamemory in young children: The role of theory of mind and metacognitive vocabulary'. *Metacognition and Learning*, 1 (1), 15–31.
Luria, A.R. (1973) *The Working Brain: An Introduction to Neuropsychology*. New York: Basic Books.
Mevarech, Z. and Fridkin, S. (2006) 'The effects of IMPROVE on mathematical knowledge, mathematical reasoning and meta-cognition'. *Metacognition and Learning*, 1 (1), 85–97.
Mitchell, P. and Riggs, K.J. (eds.). (2000) *Children's Reasoning and the Mind*. Hove, UK: Psychology Press.
Nelson, T.O. and Narens, L. (1990) 'Metamemory: A theoretical framework and new findings'. In: G.H. Bower (ed.), *The Psychology of Learning and Motivation Advances in Research and Theory* (Vol. 26). San Diego, CA: Academic Press, 125–173.
Office for Standards in Education. (2007) *Making Sense of Religion: A Report on Religious Education in Schools and the Impact of Locally Agreed Syllabuses*. London: Office for Standards in Education.
Office for Standards in Education. (2010) *Transforming Religious Education: Religious Education in schools 2006–09*. London: Office for Standards in Education.
Office for Standards in Education. (2013) *Religious Education: Realising the Potential*. Manchester, UK: Office for Standards in Education.
Perfect, T.J., and Schwartz, B.L. (eds.). (2002) *Applied Metacognition*. Cambridge, UK: Cambridge University Press.
Pett, S. (2018) 'Where do you stand? Insider and outsider views on religion in RE'. *REToday*, 2018 (Autumn), 49–55.
Piaget, J. (1975) *L'équilibration des Structures Cognitives: Problème central du développement (The Development of Thought: Equilibration of Cognitive Structures)*. Paris: PUF (Eng. trans. New York: Viking Press).
Portilho, E.M.L. and Medina, G.B.K. (2016) 'Metacognition as methodology for continuing education of teachers'. *Creative Education*, 7 (1), 1–12.
Qualifications and Curriculum Authority. (2000) *Religious Education: Non-Statutory Guidance on RE*. London: Qualifications and Curriculum Authority.

Qualifications and Curriculum Authority. (2004) *Religious Education: The Non-Statutory National Framework*. London: Qualifications and Curriculum Authority.
Reder, L. and Schunn, C.D. (1996) 'Metacognition does not imply awareness: Strategy choice is governed by implicit learning and memory'. In: L. Reder (ed.), *Implicit Memory and Metacognition*. Mahwah, NJ: Lawrence Erlbaum Associates, 45–78.
Religious Education Council of England and Wales. (2013) A review of religious education in England. Online. http://resubjectreview.recouncil.org.uk/media/file/RE_Review.pdf (accessed 7 June 2018).
Robson, S. and Flannery Quinn, S. (eds.). (2015) *The Routledge International Handbook of Young Children's Thinking and Understanding*. Oxford, UK: Routledge.
Rosch, E. (1975) 'Cognitive representations of semantic categories'. *Journal of Experimental Psychology: General*, 104 (3), 192–233.
Rosenthal, R. and Jacobson, L. (1968) *Pygmalion in the Classroom: Teacher Expectation and Pupils' Intellectual Development*. New York: Holt, Rinehart & Winston.
Santisi, G., Magnano, P., Hichy, Z. and Ramaci, T. (2014) 'Metacognitive strategies and work motivation in teachers: An empirical study'. *Procedia – Social and Behavioral Sciences*, 116, 1227–1231.
Shayer, M. and Adey, P. (eds.). (2002) *Learning Intelligence*. Buckingham, UK: Open University Press.
Sheehan, D. (2015) 'Can secondary school architecture build community, encourage working successfully and enhance well-being? Student and staff evaluations'. Unpublished DEd Psych Thesis, University of Exeter, UK, College of Social Sciences and International Studies.
Taylor, T. (2016) *A Beginner's Guide to Mantle of the Expert: A Transformational Approach to Education*. London: Singular Publishing.
Teece, G. (2010) 'Is it learning about and from religions, religion or religious education? And is it any wonder some teachers don't get it?' *British Journal of Religious Education*, 32 (2), 93–103.
Teece, G. (2011) 'Too many competing imperatives? Does RE need to rediscover its identity?' *Journal of Beliefs & Values*, 32 (2), 161–172.
Thomas, G.P. (2003) 'Conceptualisation, development and validation of an instrument for investigating the metacognitive orientation of science classroom learning environments: The Metacognitive Orientation Learning Environment Scale – Science (MOLES – S)'. *Learning Environments Research*, 6 (2), 175–197.
Thomas, G.P. and Mee, D.A.K. (2005) 'Changing the learning environment to enhance students' metacognition in Hong Kong primary school classrooms'. *Learning Environments Research*, 8 (3), 221–243.
Valk, J. (2009a) 'Knowing self and others: Worldview study at Renaissance College'. *Journal of Adult Theological Education*, 6 (1), 69–80.
Valk, J. (2009b) 'Religion or worldview: Enhancing dialogue in the public square'. *Marburg Journal of Religion*, 14 (1), 1–16.
Valk, J. (2010) 'Worldview education in a changing world'. Paper presented at the International Seminar on Religious Education and Values, Ottawa, Canada, July.
van der Zee, T., Hermans, C. and Aarnoutse, C. (2006) 'Primary school students' metacognitive beliefs about religious education'. *Educational Research and Evaluation*, 12 (3), 271–293.
Vischer, J.C. (2008) 'Towards a user-centred theory of the built environment'. *Building Research and Information*, 36 (3), 231–240.
Vygotsky, L.S. (1978 [original manuscripts ca. 1930–1934]) In: M. Cole, V. John-Steiner, S. Scribner and E. Souberman (eds.) (A.R. Luria, M. Lopez-Morillas and M. Cole [with J.V. Wertsch], trans.), *Mind in Society: The Development of Higher Psychological Processes*. Cambridge, MA: Harvard University Press.
Walshe, K. (2011) 'Using artefacts in religious education'. *The Religious Education CPD Handbook*. Religious Education Council of England and Wales: London. Online. www.re-handbook.org.uk/section/approaches/using-artefacts-in-religious-education#tab-3 (accessed 7 June 2018).
Wright, A. (2000) 'The spiritual education project: Cultivating spiritual and religious literacy through a critical pedagogy of religious education'. In: M. Grimmitt (ed.), *Pedagogies of Religious Education: Case Studies in the Research and Development of Good Pedagogic Practice in RE*. Great Wakering, UK: McCrimmons, 170–187.

Index

Page numbers in **bold** indicate tables.

academic studies of religion 5, 117, 120
activity designing 70–2; *see also* lesson planning
All-Party Parliamentary Group (APPG) on RE report 67
Ardila, A. 17
art activities: Buddhism 35
assessment 94–6, 120; problems in 3; *see also* Worldview Profiles

Baker, L. 16
Baumfield, V. 61
belief (word) 28; lesson planning and 33–5; *see also* mental state words
"Believe-it-or-not" activity 73
Beyerstein, B.L. 15
bias: acknowledging 5–6; concerns about 4, 99; impossibility of avoiding 44
Blaylock, L. 61, 94
Bloom, B. 79
board games 73–5, 103–4
Bottiroli, S. 19
boundaries 24, 60
brain structures 17
Buddhism 29; lesson planning 35–6

Carpendale, J.I. 28
Cary, M. 29–30
Chandler, D. 14
Chandler, M.J. 28
Chater, M. 61
Christmas: games about 74–5

classrooms: physical layouts for 20–2, 26; and question strategies 30; resources zones in 58, 86; space in 22, **25**, 39, 78, 86, 99; *see also* schools
Coffield, F. 15
cognitive strategies/knowledge **101**
collaboration 24, **25**, 66, 72
collective worship 111
Commission on Religious Education (2018) 1, 3–4, 57–8, 61, 67
Copley, T., 95
Crooks, S. 7

decision-making 23
Diana, R.A. 26–7
disciplinary skills 5
Dunlosky, J. 19

Easter story: and sacrifice game 103; and the "Throne" activity 76–7, 83–4
Ecclestone, K. 15
Erricker, C. 43, 61
Erricker, J. 43
Eflikides, A. 32
Elliott, A. 18

faith: discussing 104
Fancourt, N. 94–5
feeling: types of 32
feelings: expressing 32–3; metacognitive experience cards 33
Flavell, J.H. 6, 21–2, 28, 80, **101**

Flavell's theory of metacognition 6, 16, 22, 100
Fraser, B.J. 20
Fridkin, S. 18
frontal lobes (brain) 17

Graesser, A.C. 29
Greenfield, S. 15
Grimmitt, M. 43
group work 17; and physical space 22

Hall, E. 15
Hartwig, M. 19
Hatano, G. 37
Heathcote, D. 77
Hichy, Z. 105
Hinduism: and "How good is that?" activity 79–80
Homan, R. 59
"hospital chapel activity" 65–6
"How good is that?" activity 79–80

improved metacognition: benefits of 8
Inagaki, K. 37
inclusive multi-faith RE 2, 43–4, 120, 122
intended learning outcomes: problems with 3
inter-faith dialogue: Johnston on 21
Islam: "Submission impossible" activity 80–1

Jackson, R. 43
Jacobson, L. 20
Johnston, W. 21
Judaism: and the "Throne" activity 77
Juliebö, M. 18
Jurado, M.B. 17

Kelly, G.A. 105
Kelly's personal construct theory 105

Langer, E. 23
language: conditional phrases 23; and tasks 23; and young children 27
learning activities: Flavell on 23; Worldview Question Frameworks 48–9
learning environments 5, 11, 19–21
"learning from religion" 43, 61, 89
learning style categorization: and metacognition 15
Leopold, C. 18
lesson planning 12, 62–5, **66**, 117; "belief" activity 33–5; Buddhism 35–6; "hospital chapel activity" 65–6; and the resources zone 58: *see also* activity designing; specific activities/lessons
Leutner, D. 18
Lilienfeld, S.O. 15
Lily, J. 95
listening skills: developing 26, 29
Lockl, K. 27

Logan, J. 43
Lynn, S.J. 15

Magnano, P. 105
Malicky, G. 18
Medina, G.B.K. 105
Mee, D.A.K. 91
mental state words 27–9, 39, 65–6, 102
meta-communication skills 24
meta (prefix) 16
meta-thinking zone 10–12, 22, **25**, 37, 78, 87, 114–15, **122**; "belief" activity 34; goals of 26–7; knowledge cards 30, **31**; metacognitive experience cards **33**; monitoring/control cards **32**; and questions 29, 39; and RE 33; set-up for 30
metacognition 104, 115; defining 6–9, 113; demonstrating 65–6; Helen on 40; and language 27; promotion of 9–10, 78, 98–100, 113; and Religious Education 81; and self-categorization 14–15; social 24; thinking shifts 28, 37; and worldviews 9; *see also* metacognitive knowledge
metacognition workshops 18
metacognitive approach 3–4
metacognitive beliefs: influence of religion on 7
metacognitive discussions 73
metacognitive experiences 22–3, 32, **101**, 104, 115, 118
metacognitive knowledge 15–16, 26, **101**, 114, 118; cards for 30, **31**; and mental state words 27–8
metacognitive learning environments 5, 11, 23–4, **25**, 62–3, 89, 123; physical layouts for 20, 22, 26; and questions 29; teaching strategies as 19–20; thinking changes needed for 20, 24
metacognitive self-knowledge: and metacognitive teaching strategies 20
Mevarech, Z. 18
mindless learning 23
monitoring/control processes 16–17, 26–7, 31, **32**, 44
Mosley, D. 15
Muslims: "Submission impossible" activity 80–1

Narens, L. 17
National Association of Teachers of Religious Education (NATRE) 68
National Entitlement to the Study of Religion and Worldviews 61, 67–8
Nelson, T.O. 17
Norman, C. 18
non-denominational RE *see* inclusive multi-faith RE

Ofsted: 2010 report 63, 68; 2013 report 63, 67, 94
Ota, C. 43

Peacock, A. 95
Person, N.K. 29
personal construct theory 105–6
personal identity **45**, 121
Pett, S. 42
Piaget, J. 72
Portilho, E.M.L. 105
practitioners: vs. researchers 3
Priestly, J. 95
pupil assumptions 9, 41–2
pupil/pupil relationships 20, 23–4, 114
pupil-supplied objects: resource zone 58–9
pupils 89–90, 111, 119; discussing faith 104; interviewed 88–90; receptivity to questions 78–9; and "think" 28, 102; on Worldview Profiles 50–1, 92–3

questions: after activities 65; "belief" activity 34; "Believe-it-or-not" activity 73; Buddhism activity 35–6; guiding RE-flect project 8; importance to meta-thinking zone 29; metacognitive experience cards **33**; metacognitive knowledge cards 30, **31**; and metacognitive lessons 64, 114; modelling 29; monitoring/control cards **32**; religious artifacts 59–60; research studies into 29–30; Worldview Question Frameworks 45–7, 48, 50, 55–6
questions (call-out): activities 66; assessment/marking 18, 95, 100; classroom space 22; collaborative experiences 72; idea expression 104; learning from each other 103; making use of metacognitive knowledge 16; mental state words 28; opportunities for reflection 63; RE 88; reflective questions 33; resources zone 59; "Throne" activity 77; Worldview Profiles 49; Worldview Question Frameworks 48; worldviews 42

Ramaci, T. 105
RE-flect project 5–7, 57, 64, 103, 118, **122**; challenges 111–12; classroom spaces for 26, 78; goals of 8, 61, 113; learning environments 21–2; as metacognitive intervention programme 19; and metacognitive knowledge cards 31; promoting metacognition 9–10, 75, 91, 100, 113; questions guiding 8; and repertory grids 106, **107**, 108; schools involved in 85–6; sociocultural aspects of 20; structuring of 10, 12; teachers involved in 67, 70–1, 85, 96, 98, 119; teaching RE before 10; and worldviews 45
RE teachers: responsibilities of 5
RE Today Services 68
Reder, L. 26–7, 29–30
reflection 6, 114, 123; encouraging 26, 48, 62–3, 114; and monitoring/control 32; outside of RE 40; and the resources zone 60; time for 24, **25**, 123

reflective diaries 48–9, 109–10, 112; *see also* Worldview Profiles
Religious Education: assessment 3, 94–6; challenges to 1–3, 60–1, 87, 110–11, 118; and creative activities 15; and the meta-thinking zone 33; and metacognition 81, 100, 122; pre-RE-flect project 10, 118; purpose of 4–5, 42–3, 60–2, 121; requirements for 2, 23–4, 61; student motivations 19, 90; students on 88–9; teachers on 89–90, 106, 111; underestimating 80; and Worldview Profiles 51; and worldviews 9, 42
Religious Education: Non-statutory Guidance on RE (2000) 44
Religious Education Council of England and Wales 1, 67, 94
Religious Education in English Schools: Non-statutory Guidance 2010 62
Religious Education Metacognitive Orientation Scale (REMOS) 91
repertory grids 106, **107**, 108, 110, 112
research studies 7–8; factors impacting 19; into questions 29–30; of metacognition 11, 18, 27; and metacognition 122; of metacognition intervention programmes 18–19; physical environments 21–2; transfer 37–8
researchers: vs. practitioners 3
resources zone 10, 12, 22, **25**, 57, 68, 78, 114, 116–17, **122**; objects in 59; pupil-supplied objects 58–9; and reflection 60; siting 58–9
Review of Religious Education in England (2013) 67
roleplay lessons: "hospital chapel" activity 65–6; "Throne" activity 76–7, 83–4
roles: questioning 24
Rosch, E. 14
Rosenthal, R. 20
Rosselli, M. 17
Ruscio, J. 15

SACRIFICE: The Ultimate Trading Game 73–4, 103–4
Santisi, G. 105
Schunn, C.D. 26–7
safe spaces 24, **25**, 49, 81, 113–14
St. Mary's University study 7–8
Schneider, W. 27
schools 85–6; on RE 110–11; with religious character 2, 86–7; without religious character 2, 44, 86–7, 120–1; *see also* classrooms
self-assessment 95
self-awareness 24, 44, 105, 112
self-knowledge 16, 44; and metacognitive knowledge cards 31
self-monitoring 17, **101**, 115
self-regulation 8, 17–18, 30, **101**, 115
Sheehan, D. 21–2

Shoveller, S. 95
small groups: "belief" activity 34
social metacognition 24, 66, 113–14, 120, 123
Soucy, A. 7
strategies 23, **101**; and group discussions 104; and metacognitive knowledge cards 30, **31**; planning 18, 23; and questions 29–30
strategy variable 16
Struthers, D. 95
"Submission impossible?" activity 80–1
Sullivan, D. 43

task knowledge 16
task rubrics 18
tasks 23, 63; and metacognitive experiences 22–3, 63; and metacognitive knowledge cards 30, **31**
teacher/pupil relationships 20, 23–4, 78, 114, 118
teachers: Continuing Professional Development 68, 118; lack of training for 67–8, 110, 118; metacognition of 105, 109–10; modelling metacognition questions 29; online support for 68; on RE 87, 96, 98, 111; repertory grids 106, **107**, 108, 110, 112
teachers for RE 10, 110, 118
Teacher Voices 98–99; Cari 83–84; Helen 39–40; Jeanette 55–56
Teece, G. 43, 61
tests: answer types 18
The Meaning of Christmas game 74–6
theories of learning 27
theories of metacognition 11
theories of mind 28, 104

think (word) 28; *see also* mental state words
Thomas, G. 20, 91
"Throne" activity 76–7, 83–4
traffic light assessment scheme 37, 39
transfer 37–8, 104, 115
transferable skills 5

Valk, J. 45
van der Zee, T. 7, 19
verb-on-verb tools 80
Vischer, J.C. 21–2
Vygotsky, L.S. 27

Walshe, K. 19, 59–61
word clouds 51, 55
worldview education 45
Worldview Profiles 41, 48–50, 99, 116, 119–22; activities used in 51–2; concerns to consider 49; limitations of 51–2; marking/assessment/confidentiality of 49–53, 91–2, 119; pupil responses to 50–1, 92–3; teacher-provided questions in 53; teachers on 55–6, 91–2; *see also* reflective diaries
worldview profiling 8, 48–9, 75, 119–20
Worldview Question Frameworks **45–7**, 48–50, 52–4
worldview zone 10, 12, 22, **25**, 41, 56, 73, 78, 86, 114–16, **122**
worldviews 53, 92, 115; defining 9; and metacognition 9; recognising 41; shaping 42–4; and Worldview Profiles 51
Wright, A. 43
writing strategies: and metacognition 14–15